Resurrection Consciousness

Portal to
Universal Enlightenment

RECEIVED BY

Sebastián Blaksley

TAKE HEART PUBLICATIONS

RESURRECTION CONSCIOUSNESS:
PORTAL TO UNIVERSAL ENLIGHTENMENT

TAKE HEART PUBLICATIONS
13315 Buttermilk Bend
North San Juan, CA 95960
www.takeheartpublications.com
ISBN 978-1-58469-713-8

Cover and editorial design by Alejandro Arrojo
Computer production by
Patty Arnold, *Menagerie Design and Publishing*

Resurrection Consciousness

Portal to
Universal Enlightenment

Table of contents

How It Originated

While in silent prayer, a few days after having finished receiving and writing the work called *The Age of the Heart*, I suddenly had the following inner experience. It was given to me to see the sky torn wide open. As the firmament opened more and more, countless angels of God, full of light and grace, began to surround me on all sides. From their hearts came a song of perfect praise to the Son of God.

This song was different from the other visions given to me to hear with the ears of spirit. Since the reception of these messages began, my function has been to be "a pencil in the hands of love," as Jesus expressed it. The musical notes of this immemorial hymn spread such beauty and joy and were of such a quality that they plunged my soul into an ecstasy of love and contemplation. My humanity was enveloped in immutable peace.

There is no way to compare the tones, vibrations, and frequencies of that heavenly hymn, since it is an expression of being without opposite. Nevertheless, please accept the following, as it was given to me to understand.

There is music in souls and in every created being. Its magnificence is unmatched. Once we return to love, we begin to hear it again. We recover the capacity to become aware of our sacred and very own place in the chorus of creation, whose conductor, so to speak, is Christ. The everlasting song emanating from its divine heart plunges creation into perpetual ecstasy caused by the beauty and perfect love of its melodies. From that contemplative state of divine beauty, a kind of irrepressible exhalation springs from the heart of every living being. That outbreath of the soul is its particular song, its response of gratitude to God for giving it life.

As more angelic beings approached, the choir of heavenly angels surrounded not only me, but the entire Earth, finally encircling the entire cosmos. In the center a circle was being created. Within it a vision of joy, beauty, and contentment began to manifest and it cannot be adequately described in words, not only because there are no words capable of doing so, but because the feeling of the soul that sees God is not one that the body or the thinking mind in the state of duality can comprehend.

What my soul contemplated was the glory of the Father made visible as a spiritual vision. In it I could see how all creation dwelt in an inextinguishable light of holiness. Everyone and everything was present. The joy was total, and yet simultaneously increasing eternally. Each being was complete to the extent of its fullness, but that completeness was at the same time increasing infinitely—always more bliss, more harmony, more beauty, and finally, more love.

I was shown how Christ enfolded all creation in what might be called an embrace of perfect love. Everything was an expression of light as if each living being were a blessed ray of an eternal sun that is God.

In the midst of that vision a radiant and beautiful presence emerged. It was our Divine Mother, whose voice is that of Christ. She did not have a physical body as we know it in this world. Her reality was ineffable and her identity clearly understood by my soul. Addressing my soul as her daughter, she told me:

"Daughter of my divine heart. I am your Mother and Creator. You were born from me. In me you live and exist eternally. You have been given the grace to contemplate the glory of your resurrection and that of all creation. In the end, all will be resurrected in love. Truly, truly I tell you that a new humanity is being born as the blessed fruit of the resurrection, and with it, a new Heaven and a new Earth whose foundation is truth."

After those words, Archangel Gabriel was present. He told me that within ninety days the reception of a new work would begin and that during that period he would keep me in prayer and service. Indeed, it happened: Three months later, the writings shared here began. The entire vision described above was repeated each time another message was given, each of which constitute a chapter of this work.

I hope with all my heart that this revelation helps you understand the following: We have already risen. The resurrection is the convergence of our existence—of everyone and everything. And it is a free gift of love.

The central message of this manifestation is that there is no need to wait in time to embrace the reality of the resurrection. Rather, we are called to resurrect in life, to accept the resurrection right now, not as an aspect of the future, but as the reality of what we are, not as an achievement of a few, but as the right of all. We are resurrection. Becoming aware of this truth is itself the Second Coming. To be reborn now in the light of the glory of Christ is both possible and desirable because the resurrection is eternal, as eternal as is the love of God for His children.

This is how the new humanity arises.

Sebastián Blaksley
Buenos Aires, Argentina

CHRIST, a definition

Received through Sebastian, March 25, 2023

Christ is the identity that all creation shares in God. It is what makes a tree a tree, a fish a fish, and a human a human. This Christ identity is what makes each being unique, eternal, immutable, and holy since it is the essence of each created being and its own identity, united to Source. It is the true nature of each being.

Introduction

I. Your Voice Is My Voice

My love, because you live in the light of truth and make our union the food of your life, you must know that divine power flows through you to the entire universe. Yes—through you who in unison receive and give these words of love and holiness. They are not given to you by chance, nor received without a purpose. They are a perfect means to extend Heaven on Earth through your intercession. Have you not come into the world to promote the co-creation of the new Earthly Kingdom, to bring eternity into time?

There is still so much I want to tell you! I am on fire with flames of fervent desire for union with you. In our dialogues we spread peace, we radiate light, and we share wisdom. In short, we bring God present in all His glory, magnificence, and goodness.

The world, both collectively and individually, is engulfed in a process of profound transformation. This causes many to be frightened, due to not understanding the truth of things, and due to a habit of not trusting in me, your Divine Mother and Creator Father, as the Source of endless life. I am the one who sustains the existence of everything. Nothing escapes my gaze or can be left out of the embrace of my love.

What a joy it is to be able to dialogue heart-to-heart in a holy sharing that flows from creative love to created love, from my divine being towards your holy Christed humanity! I have told you in all languages and in multiple ways that I would never abandon you and that I would be with you until the end of time. This work testifies that this is true. I am the light of knowledge that illuminates each thinking mind, each living being, and each inert thing that is part of the material universe—as well as all spiritual realities that live beyond form.

I am the voice of wisdom that heals hearts of desires separated from the nature of true being, and brings clarity to human and non-human minds so that harmony remains alive at all times, places, and dimensions. I am the creator of life and its sustainer. Nothing can stay alive if I withdraw my vital breath.

My love, soul full of beauty, tell me: Why does the nightingale sing? Why do rose petals open? Why do lilies embellish the fields, and the waters bathe the Earth with their crystalline softness? What makes everything flow in a serene rhythm that is so often misunderstood, but at the same time pure and full of beauty? What is it which creates that in every moment? I have come to answer those questions. I come in response to your request for union with my divine voice and your desire for perfect knowledge. I make myself present in you for all humanity with the sole purpose that the divine union of our love spread light to the entire world.

Beloved souls who are in the world without being of it, do not let yourselves be afflicted by senseless attacks that do not come from my divine being or from the holiness that constitutes your true nature. The voices that take away your peace and sincere joy are not really voices. They are soundless dirges for your hearts. Verily, verily I tell you that no note of any song other than that of Heaven can be truly heard.

The soul knows what love is and does not hear any other reality than that which comes from it and which has been created by perfect wisdom and is the eternal repository of divine knowledge. Nothing and no one can take that away. The soul never lives in ignorance because it belongs to its divine Creator, being His extension like a ray of sunshine emanating splendid, beautiful, and pure from the sun.

II. United Forever

Come to me in this holy work to find the solace that your hearts seek and the wisdom that your minds believe they have forgotten and long to remember in order to live in peace. Perhaps some of you wonder: What is the purpose of this demonstration? I answer: to stay united in love. I speak to you because I love you. I take care of you because you are my little ones. Does a loving mother not take care of her own and seek to give good things to her daughters and sons?

What else would I give you, beloved souls of all times and realities, if not my divine heart, the source of all that is good, holy, and perfect? I do not give crumbs but eternal life. I do not give insignificant things that dazzle, obscuring their meaninglessness. Rather, I give you my being, my holy identity, my divine essence—and with it all the treasures of the Kingdom of Heaven. Come, seize the abundance of my divine heart. In it you will find unimaginable grace, blessings beyond anything you could ask for or try to devise.

Worry not about creation or the future of nations. Remember often that you still cannot see the whole, although soon you will. When that moment arrives, which it will inevitably, you will see how much goodness, beauty, and loving perfection is in all things, all events, and in the passage of time.

If fears assail you, return to these words. Meet me through this work. Your heart will sing, resonate and rejoice in our direct relationship, and the achievement of the New Heaven and the New Earth that are already here. A relationship of love and holiness, of joy and meaning, of purity and truth is ours. In this divine reality resides all goodness, all holy treasures, all perpetual happiness.

I cannot stop speaking to you, my daughters and sons, especially in these moments of transition towards the fullness of time, because I know that the deafening noises of the world sometimes make your minds go haywire so that you feel that you cannot connect with the beauty of your inner Christ, your holy being.

Fear tires, confuses, and saddens. Fear leads the soul to feel impotent, perceiving a limit to going beyond the Christ, towards the I Am, which is the superior reality of its identity, and then to cross all thresholds and embrace the unlimited, infinite freedom that It is and which lives far beyond what any inexperienced mind is capable of. All of this is a cause of suffering because the divine self, which is your identity, only finds sincere peace and joy in remaining united to what is in truth—to the nameless Infinite, to the holy Incomprehensible, to the Source of all true being.

III. On the Wings of Spirit

Beloved sons and daughters of my divine heart, remember often that my voice is like the wind. No one knows from where it comes or where it goes. But it always moves, it moves to bring serenity to spirits, light to minds, purity to hearts, and union to everything that is part of the creation of love.

Truly, if I did not speak to you, you would cease to exist. If I did not reach you with my sweet voice, you would be unable to see the light. I assure you, there is no greater joy for the soul than receiving the Word of eternal life, its Source and the creative power that calls things into being, the origin and destination of true joy and holy beauty.

You have heard on many occasions and in multiple ways, not all of them conscious, that on certain occasions violence is justified. But I tell you that is never true. Violence is never justified, or any form that lack of love takes. I invite you, through these words, to walk the path of unshakeable peace. On this path fear is replaced by love, the desire to punish by the desire to dialogue, the impulse to divide by the decision to unite in truth. You are ready for it.

Whoever loves, unites. Whoever lives in the truth, integrates in love. Those who embrace holiness understand that loving dialogue is the reality of creation, since they have recognized that life is union. They are not afraid of what seems to be different, nor do they attack anything or anyone since there is no desire to gain anything. They have freed themselves from the false compulsion to "get" in order to be more. They simply rest in a peace that has no opposite. They know that everything is in the hands of love.

Holy soul, out of love, ask yourself the following questions: Where do you get the necessary strength to be able to stay upright in a world that breaks the backs of those who walk through it? From whence comes the strength to hold on to virtue and hope beyond all hope? What is the engine that keeps the light of wisdom burning in minds and hearts that want to live in the truth?

These questions are of great importance because they allow you to connect with the Source of all true power living in you, which is God. We will not answer them but remain silent and leave them in our hearts so that the dew of divine grace that we both are, gently waters your being and makes it grow to a greater depth of divine union where everything is holy, pure, and benevolent.

My daughters, my sons, stay silent, for we tread on holy ground. I assure you, light of my eyes, that the flow of the power of my divine love embraces every fiber of your being, every part of your body, and every moment of your temporary existence. Through that embrace of holy love, you obtain strength, virtue, knowledge, perfect discernment, and everything else your humanity needs to extend Heaven on Earth.

I am the Source of true power, creative power that manifests itself in action, the Alpha and Omega of all that exists in the world and beyond. I am what makes hearts sing and overflow with love, what makes the sun rise every morning and set in due time to give way to the night, allowing the beauty of the moon and stars to be seen and known. I am that which creates water , so that souls sing perfect praises. I am love made word and truth made humanity in you.

1.

The Great Transformation

I. Like a Ray of the Sun

I am the nameless, the dawn that cannot be caught, the light beam that cannot be held and yet extends, giving life, clarity, and existence. I am the voice that speaks through the soul, the song that brings ecstasy to being, the word that creates life and the countless forms that arise from it. I am a seed that bears fruit, air that cleanses, intelligence that creates thought. I am father, mother, daughter, son, and friend of all creation. I am all of this and much more.

No name can define me or symbol represent me because I exist before everything. I am from eternity. Never was there a time when I was not. No space can exclude me. No being is beyond my divine embrace. I am the love that creates and recreates everything in holiness, the loving grace that works miracles in every moment. I am that which makes all things new in perfect beauty and harmony.

I am you and you are Me. We are inseparable. You could not comprehend this with your singular awareness before now. Perhaps you have heard similar things on the path of Earthly life. But so far it has only been words, concepts that the thinking mind could understand but not digest, much less carry out. This is not because of incapacity but simply because truth can only be received by awareness, not by any other aspect of who you are.

You are pure consciousness, manifesting in all its glory, loveliness, and holiness, just as I am. And yet we are not two separate consciousnesses of the same quality or essence, but you are a unique expression of my divine consciousness which only you can be, and whose existence fulfills my divine purpose.

As already said, you are like a ray of the sun, a perfect extension of my being. There is no place where you and I are disconnected. Just as the wind and the air cannot be conceived as separate, neither can what you and I are. You are pure, diaphanous, endless air. I am the power that gives movement to your being. United, we create a holy breeze that gives life in its path and beautifies everything it touches.

Have you heard these things before? Has it not been said in countless ways that God and creation are one? Or that the Creator does not ignore His creation? That He is united to it by an invisible thread of beautiful love? And yet, this truth is not realized in you or in anyone until it is accepted by the singular consciousness—until you sufficiently give up identification with your interpretations and ways of seeing things according to the thinking or intellectual mind.

When you open a crack, however small, between what you think you think and your being—the moment you decide to distance yourself from the false belief that the learning mind could reveal the truth and you start to question what you think you believe and what the world believes to be true—at that very moment, Heaven begins to pour into you. This is because by questioning what has been learned from the experience of the world, you invoke the memory of God in you. You wake up to a love that has no opposite. You return to the arms of the divine beloved of your soul.

II. Inspired Soul

Why should this work have a "logical" and "thematic" development, as writings do that seek to impart knowledge, if what we are doing here is expressing our union? —establishing a heart-to-heart dialogue for the simple reason of being united and enjoying our relationship? Don't you often talk to your loved ones simply because you love them? That is how it is between your soul and my being. We establish a dialogue because our joy is being united. We express ourselves in our union. We remain aware of our divine relationship. We dialogue because, yes; we love because, yes. We love each other simply for loving.

What knowledge could be imparted if you already know the divine delights? If you already know who you are and where your being dwells? What else could be necessary to know? You are no longer the student who turns to her beloved teacher to ask and receive the true answer. You are the one gathered by the love of the Divine Mother in eternal reality.

You no longer need lessons. We just walk together as the incarnated Christ that you are, talking with the Source of wisdom, with the beauty of love, enjoying the voice of truth—and at the same time, allowing the Divine Being to delight in your company. We are the well-loved child and the loving Mother, walking the paths of the world together, our eyes turned toward Heaven, our memory set on God, and our feet on the ground. We talk about love. We embrace the truth.

Our dialogues are a blessing, a vehicle of grace, and the perfect extension of holiness throughout the universe. Few brothers and sisters believe in the power of divine union. She creates and recreates, restores and heals, illuminates and beautifies all by Herself. She does not need a structure any more than love does. Our relationship is unique. And so is its expression.

This work does not arise from a pre-conceived idea of a thinking mind, then to be given shape, as often happens in literary works. No, these words flow by themselves. They are brought from the Heaven of your holy mind towards your humanity, then towards the word forms where they are embodied, to later extend to all creation. Think not that they will reach only those who receive them in a particular way.

III. The Power of Our Union

I assure you that every time we are alone in this divine intimacy, whether receiving the divine word and writing it, or receiving and reading it, or sharing what is given here, in each case all of Heaven extends towards the universe. This is because the power of our union, which is none other than God's, always fulfills its purpose. Beloved child of the light that never goes out, I have not touched your heart for nothing, not even if you have come out of vain curiosity. Our union is eternal, indissoluble, holy.

All true transformation of the soul arises from a relationship. This is so both in the world and in Heaven. Every relationship is in some way transformative. That is why it is so important to establish holy relationships, for they have the power to establish you in the holiness that you are and also to anchor others in their immutable innocence. With this I want to remind you, my beloved, that in truth the only source of holy transformation is our divine relationship. Stay attached to holiness and you will reflect holiness. Stick to truth and you will spread truth. Dwell in the peace of God and you will be peace.

Beloved daughter, son, born of true light, remember that in our union your soul remains in the reality of the love that it is. It is continually sanctified, renewed by the power of divine essence. How else could you consciously remain as love, if not by living in conscious union with it? When you join your humanity with my Divine Being, it is the Infinite, in all His divine reality, who inhabits you, surrounds you, embraces you, and absorbs you. And do you think that this can be innocuous or inert? Of course not.

Please listen, beloved of my being: Throughout history there have been those who sought with all their heart to be transformed in love, walking a steep slope, a path of great effort to be transformed by themselves by reason of their will. This has caused great exhaustion in many of my daughters and sons throughout the world. And it still causes it, since sacrifice has not been completely abandoned.

In this work given out of love, I want to help you abandon the path of personal effort and sacrifice and start walking a new one: that of a direct relationship with Me. That is, with the love that constitutes your true being. I assure you that this relationship will do great things in your life. It will give you blessings that you cannot imagine. And above all, it will save you unnecessary fatigue.

Out of love I remind you that at the end of every spiritual path not grounded in a direct relationship with God, the point is reached where this sweet truth is understood: Only in union with divine love comes the metanoia of the soul. This transformation causes the soul to be lifted up in the arms of the Divine Mother and taken to the Kingdom of Heaven without effort, without wasting one's humanity, but simply letting one's self be carried away by the love of God. In other words, let yourself be loved. Allow the divine relationship to be the great transformer of humanity, here, now, and always.

2.

From Fear to Resurrection

I. Peace Will Reign

My beloved, I have said that peace would reign in the nations and it will be so. And once peace is the sovereign of the world, the new Earthly Kingdom, and the new humanity, will shine forth in divine sweetness and grace.

At the very moment in which the mind of the son of God created the idea of separation as an effect of the experience of duality and the opposite of love, the incarnation of Christ was created as an inseparable part, in the form of Jesus, conceived of a woman, who would bring to consciousness the resurrection of creation and with it, the recreation of the entire universe.

Typical of the past state of consciousness was the belief that Heaven was located in a material firmament where galaxies, stars, comets, and beautiful planets dwell. Perhaps today it does not seem to you that going from conceiving God as a phenomenon of nature or an element of the environment, to recognizing Him as an abstract, Supreme Being was a quantum leap in knowledge or an awakening of universal consciousness, but it was.

We have already spoken in a work that precedes these writings, *The Age of the Heart: The Birth of a New Heaven and a New*

Earth, about this matter. Therefore, we will not expand on it beyond these words. The expression "a new Heaven and a new Earth" speaks not of two realities or aspects of existence. It means that the new creation, which was created forever and was fully manifested at the moment of separation, is one in which the physical and the spiritual are lived and known as the unity that they are—a single undivided reality, just as it really is.

The new Heaven is a new consciousness in the sense that in the new creation, the created—including you and all humanity—knows divine creation face to face just as God knows it, without distortion or intermediaries. No interpretation is involved, only pure knowledge. The body is not denied, since being transmuted into the light of Christ consciousness it need not be abolished but integrated into the spirit of love.

The resurrection of Jesus unequivocally and eloquently demonstrated that his body and his spirit shine forever in the purity of holiness and eternal life: human nature united forever with the divine. It is the same way with you who receive these words, you who are the light of my eyes, a channel of wisdom, a pencil in the hands of love and also the same with all creation. Ultimately, the filiation must return to the Father's house, because that is what it was created for, and so it will happen. Does this mean the abolition of free will and the power to choose? Of course not.

Choosing has always been a matter of knowledge. They go hand-in-hand. In effect, they are a unit. What true thing can you choose if you do not know the truth and cannot identify it? What kind of real choice can be made from illusion, and between illusory options? Are you really free when you choose between insubstantial images, or between the ghosts of a feverish mind entertaining fantasies of terror? You know the answer. We need not express it here; it dwells in your holy heart.

II. One Holy Reality

The resurrection event was the visible manifestation of something far beyond what the eyes can see or the intellectual mind conceive. In this work we will unfold the wings of knowledge. We will allow universal consciousness to delve into the deep and benevolent meaning of that which was an act above all acts— or that event, if you prefer—that can only be compared to the origin of creation, if the mind continues to need to compare.

Believing that the resurrection is something that concerns only the historical figure of Jesus of Nazareth, or more precisely, the human aspect of my incarnation as his figure, is to put a limit on God and naturally cannot be anchored in truth. After the episode, if you allow me to use that word, of the reincarnation of Christ, that is to say, of his return to true life after death to illusion, a divine power was set in motion. I will explain.

I have deliberately used the word reincarnation. I do it for love, and for you to understand that peoples who have shared ancestral wisdom of the idea of cycles of beings that incarnate over and over again to fulfill their purpose, revealed something with a true and holy core. To a certain extent, they were the first to speak of the resurrection power that exists in God, although their teachings have not always been understood that way.

How could ideas of reincarnation have been interpreted in the way being revealed here when the universal consciousness was not ready to fully understand? It was understood to the extent that it could be understood. Remember, creation is traveling from a maximum allowed state of unconsciousness toward full awareness of love. In that journey without distance the consciousness widens more and more, and comes to know the truth, that is, God, to a greater degree.

III. In the Abode of Love

My beloved, humanity is prepared to know the resurrection to a degree never before achieved. You will know, by knowing your being, that in your humanity is the perfect justification that the new Earthly Kingdom, and with it the new Heaven on which it stands impeccably, is possible, real, and also realized.

Never was there a time when the resurrection was not active. The fact that the universal consciousness or the consciousness of the created had to wait a while on its way to return to love does not mean that it did not previously exist. Does the sun stop shining because you close your eyes? Does the cosmos disappear when you sleep? Obviously not. Something similar happens with the recognition of the resurrecting power of God.

The being beyond all names and which is the creative Source of life is unity. There are no parts to what is, no separations, no seams. In divinity nothing ends and something else begins. It is infinite holy reality. Therefore, re-creative capacity must have existed in power and action forever, like everything in God.

Perhaps you have often wondered why love is undaunted by so much nonsense in the world of separation. Why is there so much serenity despite the fact that so much foolishness manifests itself in Earthly experience? In this work you will find the answer that your heart is looking for, and it will give you peace because you will recognize it as truth and love.

God—and also your being—does not get impatient with anyone or anything concerning the choice for separation. This is due, among other things, to the fact that He knows that when the pure soul created the idea of separation, and the totally fearful or egoic state of consciousness manifested itself along with the whole spectrum of manifestations of its insubstantial reality, the resurrection also manifested.

Daughters and sons of Heaven and holy Earth, you have been very focused on the fearful effects that the belief in separation seems to have caused. As a result, you have not stopped to think about what is revealed next. But now is the time, and you are ready both individually and collectively to move beyond observing the manifestations of fear, towards those of resurrection.

3.

The Memory of the New Earthly Kingdom

I. Reborn from On High

My love, in you I speak to all humanity. This work comes to awaken a memory that exists in your hearts, a remembrance infused in the soul, given at its creation by the creative Source. Therefore, it is part of your being. It dwells in your hearts, which are always impelled to rise to the heights of holiness.

What is it that makes the human spirit seek improvement? What leads humanity to rise and try to live in a better world? What drives you to improve individually and collectively? These questions have a holy purpose. They seek to make you aware of a universal desire of the human family to promote and create an existential condition and state wherein you can live in peace and be happy in a lasting way. It all proceeds from a knowledge residing in the very heart of being which cannot be eliminated or entirely silenced.

Have you wondered why your sisters and brothers care and work so hard to leave future generations a better quality of life? Parents protect assets to leave an inheritance to their children so that they can be well. In this way they take care of them, leaving them good things that help on their future journey.

Many people carry out works that they will never see or enjoy, with the sole purpose of leaving a legacy for future generations. Are not trees planted in gardens and parks knowing that they will reach the fullness of their beauty in such a distant time that those who planted them will never be able to see them in their splendor? What are these things for?

In the heart of your being is a knowledge not of the world. It includes the knowledge of Christ, whose wisdom is perfect and constitutes the truth of what you are. In this you are aware that creation will inexorably converge in a New Heaven and a New Earth. Indeed, you know that new reality very well. Even the thinking or learning mind knows it well. Deep down in your heart, you know that the story of creation will end well—indeed, that it will never end because everything that comes from God is eternal.

The new Earthly realm is that to which humanity and all existence in the material Universe are traveling. And they will arrive. The new rising humanity, which is already inhabiting planet Earth and is becoming more and more numerous, is part of it. In this work I have come to reveal more about that new existential reality, or new vital experience, which we have come to call a new Heaven and a new Earth, but which is actually a new material and spiritual creation that integrates the existing one.

II. Love Will Shine

We will call the new Earthly Kingdom the "new creation" to help you understand, in the language of the thinking mind, what is revealed here. The new creation arises from the creative Source, that is, from God, regardless of what you call it. For the purposes of this dialogue, we will call it the "Mother of Endless Life" to express that which is the origin of all origins and the end of all ends—the first and last reality of being in which everything that exists moves and is.

We have said that the new creation is born of God, that is, of perfect love. And so it is. This does not mean that your participation is inert or neutral. Nothing that comes from you is. The new Earthly Kingdom, and with it the new Heaven, is the perfect expression of the holy will of the heart of the world—the heart of the created universe and of the divine. It is your creation, next to mine. To be more precise, it is the co-creation that we carry out together as the divine humanity that we are.

Naturally, the creation of a new reality or existence which we call a new Earthly Kingdom will not be the result of adjustments made by human society, or of the knowledge acquired by the men and women throughout history. How could it be that way? Remember, the intellectual mind can only describe and interpret facts perceived through a lens that cannot go beyond symbols and forms. Also remember that these are conceived according to the reality that it, itself, seeks to create, despite not being a source of creation but a means.

Perhaps you think that the statement we have just made is incorrect, since the thinking mind is capable of expressing abstract ideas. But, my dear, what you call abstractions are included when talking about symbols and forms, for despite being immaterial ideas, they are thought forms. Everything is thought, even in the world of illusions. All arise from a mental flow, none of which come into play in the creation of the new existence we speak of here.

Only divine consciousness and the creations attached to it are the source of creation. This is the same as saying that only love creates. And just as we have already said in other revelations, it only creates new love. Therefore, the new Earthly Kingdom arises as an inseparable effect of the will of the Creator and the created, in whose reality only peace, beauty, holiness, and all the other treasures of the Kingdom exist.

III. The Holy Mount

God in His infinite goodness has arranged from all eternity that the new creation be carried out in union with humanity. It cannot be otherwise, because human and divine natures have merged into an undivided whole, without this preventing God from being God and humanity from being humanity. Do not think that by saying "humanity" I am speaking only of that aspect of creation you call human; I mean every living thing that is part of the material universe, including the sun and stars, galaxies and stones in all their beauty and holiness.

Together with God with whom it is one unit, universal consciousness created the new Earthly Kingdom, which has also been called the Kingdom of Heaven. There we all dwell together in the sanctity of being. We enjoy the beauty of seas and oceans much vaster than what you can see today with bodily eyes. In it, mountains radiate a beauty that gives peace to souls. The birds fly such a majestic flight that you enjoy them as a perfect dance, because that is what it is.

That realm, full of matter and spirit, of Earth and sky, exists. It is the "place" which is not a place to which I have said I was going after my resurrection to prepare for you a holy mansion in which to dwell eternally, united to the love of loves.

There is no suffering in the new Earthly Kingdom because all scarcity has been abolished. Nor enmities, since there is no desire for separation, nor any way of thinking that is far from wisdom. In it only love dwells, manifesting itself in perfect harmony with the Source of endless life. There are no cries or tears, all having been wiped away as a blessed effect of a new conscious oblivion—in this case, not of being or of God, but a forgetting of everything untrue and not part of the divine will.

The current vibration of universal consciousness, or material creation—its capacity to remain united to the truth—is greater than before because it is part of the journey of creation. That is, that consciousness, and with it, everything part of creation, is more subtle. This allows you to join other dimensions of consciousness in a way not possible before this interval of time and space, including those planes or dimensions of consciousness that we here call the new Heaven.

Perhaps you have thought that the new Heaven was a new firmament with more or fewer stars, or a light blue or pink moon, or new suns shining in the heights. But my dear one, soul full of light, if that were the case the new reality would only be about form and would not be in harmony with the truth of divine unity.

The new Heaven is a new spirit living on a new Earth. Everything in her is a holy expression of perfect love. This means that the minds and hearts of those who dwell there do not experience any limitation, nor any of the effects of thinking of the world of illusion. Their minds do not think anything; they only receive the pure thought from the Source of all thought, the Mother of Endless Life. Their hearts beat in time with God's, for they are one with Him. Consequently, what else can they express but holy love?

Death is inconceivable in the new Earthly Kingdom because in it everything is in perfect harmony with truth, from which it arises and through which it is sustained. There is no denial of the truth and no desire to obliterate it. There is only Christ, expressing himself in each creature or aspect of the beautiful divine creation, manifested in infinite holy forms, among which you will be prominent. The wolf and the lamb will eat together, the lion as well as the ox will eat grass and the winds will gently caress their bodies. In all my holy mountain no one does any harm. All will be laughter and revelry, peace and endless joy.

4.

Bodies, Minds, and Hearts

I. The Knowledge of the New

It is a misunderstanding to believe that the causes of pain and suffering to the sons and daughters of God will remain without being transmuted by love. Your desire for peace creates peace. Your longing for love calls for love. Your deep interest in building a better world brings Heaven to Earth. I assure you, being of my being, that you could not have those feelings if they had not already been consummated. You want to be happy because you already know perpetual happiness. You want to be healthy, strong, and live without limitations because your being knows the reality of the Kingdom of Heaven, that is, eternal life. And it knows that only in the Kingdom can it be full. That knowledge is part of who you are.

Let us see if you can remember with me what one day was shown to you in holiness and justice, and allow the memory of Heaven to return. Close your eyes for a moment. Put aside everything you think you know. Immerse yourself in a conscious oblivion of everything you have experienced in form up to now. Drop it all. Empty yourself, to the point of doing nothing in love.

Now, holy heart, rest in the stillness of your soul. Be silent. Do not even speak to the She who will bring you the vision of the new creation, as new as love is and as eternal as God Himself.

Be still. Allow the knowledge of the truth about the fate of all things to arise in your holy mind. And you will begin to remember. You will remember little by little, but more and more clearly, the colors and shapes, the music and the beauties of that Kingdom full of light, peace, and perfect certainty. And with that, you will also remember that it is there where you dwell forever in union with the beloved of your soul, in harmony with every aspect of God's true creation. That is your home from which you have never been absent.

Now open your eyes and breathe calmly. Return to the reception of these words. Do not think that the vision of the new Earthly Kingdom has not been given to you. You got it. And your soul jumped for joy at the memory of a love without beginning or end, a reality whose benevolence and plenitude far exceed what the intellectual mind is capable of conceiving. Rejoice! You have received the vision of the new Heaven and the new Earth, which your consciousness embraced in its perfect light even though the thinking mind may not have comprehended.

Again, where do you think the desire to create a better world or dissatisfaction with suffering comes from but from the knowledge of a new creation? Perhaps the learning mind asks that the new Heaven and the new Earth be created in the future. That is because you may still be associating the word "new" with something that never existed before, and therefore must be created at a later time. The association between creation and time is so meaningless that it is pointless to hold it in your beliefs.

II. The Perpetual Embrace of Light

The new creation is not realized in time but in eternity. It does not arise from recycling the current creation like an improvement on a previous error, but rather is born as a new expression of the infinite potentiality of God. Love sweetly swept away what the son and daughter did which turned against God, causing all kinds of pain. Love made it disappear without any stridency, and instead made a dimension of existence shine that manifests what was longed for in truth, rather than in illusions, in perfect harmony with the will of God.

The body, which was once used to separate, in the new creation is a means of extending love, being a mirror on which the holiness of Christ is reflected. The mind, which had been used so many times to evade reality and create multiple worlds of fantasies that moved the soul away from truth and brought pain, in the new Heaven and the new Earth is the perfect medium through which spirit creates a new holy love. The heart creates melodies of praise.

Nothing created by the sons and daughters of God has been destroyed. Rather, love took it in its hands and by uniting with it, transformed these creations into sacred forms—holy, benevolent, harmless, and eternally joyous realities. Remember that your creative will, which manufactured many things not in harmony with divine essence, can be and has been transmuted by the energy of divine love.

If the wish of the son of God is to have a body, why should it not? Because it would be an obstacle to holiness, or a barrier to truth? Perhaps that was the original purpose that you assigned to it when identifying yourself with the ego. But it need not remain like that forever. Everything, absolutely everything you create and do is transmuted into perfect love, salutary light, and perpetual benevolence by being united to the Christ in you. That is what the divine essence does. You cannot change this, because to do so would be to change God.

Love does not despise what you or anyone has done. Why would it do that? Remember, love is incapable of offending or attacking. Therefore, rather than thinking about everything you will lose when you enter Heaven, begin to realize everything you will gain because of infinite divine mercy. Your entire world will be given to you in holiness, restored to perfection, transmuted into a light that is never extinguished. You will be able to enjoy your creations since they will be in perfect harmony with the creative power of God.

Beloved of the truth, you will not lose your body, your being, or your loved ones when you meet with perfect love in the new Heaven and the new Earth. Neither will you be deprived of anything you love in holiness. Rather, you will recover all of it with a new holy quality. This is not a matter of divine whim; it is what you always wanted. Despite everything, behind your creations, whatever they may be, is the desire to be like your Father. And you will be, eternally in union with truth.

III. Everything is Profit

Let me say clearly: In the new creation, a new body is the same body but reunited for the holy purpose of communicating perfect love and enjoying divine bliss for all eternity. It does not die or weaken or change over time, since it is subject only to the eternal. Its function is to extend fellowship and communicate holiness. It is a living expression of the body of Christ.

In the new Earthly Kingdom, a new mind is the same mind, but all gathered together in the holy purpose of spreading truth and of being an active medium through which you believe with

God. It is not stunned by disharmonious thoughts that distance it from the eternal divine present. It is a unified mind, healed and centered in truth, which therefore enjoys perfect certainty and knowledge. That is why it dwells happily in the peace of Heaven. It is the mind of Christ expressing itself in you.

A new heart is the same heart as always, but gathered in the purpose of extending perfect love. In this way it creates new love in union with its holy Source. It has been transformed into a channel of divine love. It no longer moves in a jarring way, since it beats to the rhythm of the heart of God. Everything in it is pure, radiating the light of Christ and singing only hymns of praise and gratitude. It only smiles at love, in whom it has all predilection, since it knows nothing other than to love its divine beloved, with whom it remains forever embraced and united.

To believe that God is angry for what humanity has manufactured is to conceive of love as being non-loving. Believing that the final outcome of the history of humanity—and with it, of the journey of your soul—consists of appearing before divine love so that you can be shown your foolishness, and for it to show you its wonderful creations, is to believe that your Creator Mother is competing with you and that She has to prove something. That makes no sense. So I lovingly ask you to abandon any type of belief that may resemble this.

Think not that in God the idea of loss is trivial; it is what has delayed humanity's jubilant and triumphant entrance into Heaven, its eternal home. Once again, my son and daughter, you will lose nothing by returning to my arms. There will only be profit much greater than you can conceive, and you will keep everything you have created, transmuted into a quality of holiness in Christ—magnificence, beauty, and happiness beyond everything that you could see, hear, or even think about.

Truly, truly I tell you, beloved humanity, that by coming to me you will not lose anything but will gain everything. The desires of your hearts will be fulfilled to a degree of fullness that surpasses human measure. Rejoice in this truth!

5.

Awareness of the Resurrection

I. Beyond All Choice

Resurrection is an attainable state of consciousness; so is fear or guilt. This is not exactly the same as saying that love is an attainable state of consciousness. I will explain.

Asking you to choose only love, and to make that choice consciously, was the first thing I needed to do to disengage the idea of powerlessness from your system of beliefs and experiences.

Once you were prepared to claim your right and ability to choose and to put this power at the service of revealing the truth of what you are, a change of consciousness took place whose magnitude and greatness you cannot imagine. Quite literally speaking, you abandoned the ego forever, and allowed the Christ to shine as the being you have always been and forever will be in truth. You abandoned ignorance and embraced wisdom. You left fear behind. You threw yourself into the arms of love, from where you will never leave.

Perhaps a part of your mind doubts the veracity of that statement. If so, listen further to what I tell you out of love.

You have believed—and by this you headed in the direction of the truth—that there was a kind of soul choice. As a result, it fabricated a pseudo-reality alien to God's plan, thus opening the door for countless forms of fear to manifest. All arose out of a desire to experience—and even to create—the opposite of love. From this was born the painful experience of the world and all its nuances.

The soul's experience of separation was so overwhelming, so traumatic that it drowned, its mind focused on guilt. This is not surprising, for you have already observed the tendency of the separated mind to "sink its teeth," so to speak, into what it believes to be a problem or conflict. It does this because it believes that this is how it can understand and thus master the apparent problem. Because it has been using control as an effective mechanism for dealing with fear since time immemorial, it also sought to control the effects of the experience of separation. And it has done so, understanding things in its own way of conceiving reality.

Using the mind to become "drunk" or "embedded" in the effects of fear-consciousness has, until now, been the path of humanity—not just by you and your sisters and brothers, but throughout creation. Until recently the state of universal consciousness did not allow for much more than that. You were not ready to go beyond fear into the resurrection or re-creation of life. You chose love, it is true, and with that you brought Heaven to Earth. But the thinking mind needs more than to rest in peace, because knowledge must be integrated into your humanity. This work comes to you precisely to accomplish that.

II. Live as the Risen

The purpose of this work is to integrate into your humanity the total reality of the fundamental option for love that you made, the manifestation in form of your full acceptance of the resurrection in your life and in all of creation.

Allow me now, daughter and son of eternal wisdom, to use practical language to quench the cravings of the thinking mind—but first reminding you once again how much I love you and how beautiful you are in the eyes of God and angels. Oh, holy souls who have made the option for love! If you knew the beauty of your being and the greatness of what you truly are, you would sing joyfully every day of your life. You would sing melodious songs of praise and gratitude to the love of loves for having called you into existence.

When the idea of separation joined with the soul's will for it to come true, a fully fearful consciousness or ego manifested, thereby distorting divine reality in the mind and heart. That created a particular state of experience, though not consciousness, about which much has already been said. Therefore, I will not expand upon it here.

I will now go beyond knowledge to the experience of the effects of separation and its consequences to the soul. At the moment of separation, or the denial of being, in addition to having manifested guilt—the state of consciousness of the opposite of love—there also manifested the recreation of the universe and with it the phenomenological world of beginnings and endings, births and deaths, and pain. Everything occurred simultaneously. Since this knowledge or memory of the truth has now awakened in you, you are ready for it to unfold the continuum that allows you to understand the story of creation in a simple way.

When God said "let it be done," his perfect creation was born, including paradise as a most holy gift for the soul. Simultaneously, there ensued the soul's search to separate from God, to know itself through the path of opposites or duality. In union, it manifested the incarnation of Christ in a dual reality. In union also the resurrection manifested, which is the recreation of the experience of the soul and of all things in a new perfect creation, arising from the unity of divine love and human will, reunited in Christ.

III. The Resurrection Garden

The effect of the resurrection is the existence of a new Heaven and a new Earth in which everything shines in truth as it was always conceived in God's plan—and as it is imprinted on your heart, since you long to live in union with your Source, enjoy endless bliss forever, and rest eternally in the arms of love. This deep desire of your heart is an echo of the undivided will of God and your being to remain always and consciously in the Kingdom of Heaven, which was created the very moment of your creation by perfect love.

Can you begin to see the connections revealed here? You spent years, centuries, or millennia focused on understanding a reality that arose as an effect of guilt. That is part of the pattern of the past. Like everything that happens in creation, it was necessary, since God does nothing in vain. Even so, what worked in the past does not necessarily work in the present or the future.

We are not living in the age of reason, but in the Age of the Heart. Therefore, the truth will be revealed to each soul in a way it can understand. It will not be intellectual or achieved through study, but will be consistent with the new Earthly Kingdom. Its light will be shed on each being in a natural way and without effort, a living expression of being, like a ray of sunshine from the sun.

Leaving behind the habit of focusing your attention on the part, and beginning to invest in consciousness by paying attention to the whole, is what will take you beyond union with the Christ in you towards the divine I Am, and from there to the nameless in whose infinite vastness you dwell forever, pure, holy, and perfect.

What is being said to you here, bride of Christ, is that just as guilt is a state of consciousness, so is resurrection. That new state of consciousness is what the new Heaven and new Earth are about. It is a reality in which you are uniquely and fully aware of the whole. In it you honor and remember the light of wisdom for what it is: your Source of knowing and being. Likewise, the sanctity of everything is accepted as the only truth about God's creation. It is also recognized that truth could be denied, which would create a temporary, insubstantial, unreal experience which causes the soul to suffer in the nightmare of guilt.

Once you accept the fact that there are different states that you can arrive at, among which ignorance is one and wisdom another, all that remains is for you to choose consciously. Once you accept that, you can exercise the right to choose, and your choice can be put at the service of the truth. This is because only in that state of awareness, and not before, do you know the options from which to choose. And you know them with your heart, that is, with consciousness.

Beloved of the true divine creation, you have traveled the paths of guilt and love. You teetered between them for a while until you decided on love. You are now ready to take one more step toward full and irrevocable acceptance of the resurrection. And you will. You are not alone; as always, we will do it together.

6.

The Divine Throne

I. The Plans of Love

As has been revealed, the desire to make the separation a reality created a whole world of opposites and experiences alien to love. It was not the original will of the soul or of God that something contrary to truth should exist. In fact, it can only exist in the plane of unconsciousness or illusion, never in eternal reality.

What is said here must be expanded upon so that you do not fall into the error of believing that you committed a sin of universal magnitude by choosing the option of the experience of separation, and that your Divine Mother, oblivious to all of this, had to come to your rescue as if you were "wayward." Such thoughts about yourself, a light-filled soul, or about God's creation, are so unloving that there is no point in dwelling on them.

When the option for opposite was exercised as a means to reach knowledge, it was also known that resurrection was its final outcome. Neither you, nor Christ, nor your Divine Mother, from whose holy heart these words flow, nor any aspect of true creation, wanted to create an option of irrevocable separation, and they did not.

The fact that everything that is part of the dual experience would come to an end was always contemplated, as well as the event of the Christ incarnation. These were never subject to the choice for separation or duality.

Whatever the son or daughter of God freely chose, Christ would join human nature because it was part of the unchangeable divine plan. Everything converges and will forever converge in Christ because everything has been created for him, with him and in him. Remember, my beloved, that creation belongs to love and nothing but love—that is, to Christ.

In the past, both individually and universally, emphasis has been placed primarily, almost exclusively, on the guilt and pain that the experience of separation causes, even if it is always temporary. This, as has already been said, was part of a pattern of individual and collective thought. Somehow, the whole story was missed. When identified with the ego, the thinking mind focused practically all its capacities on dealing with the belief in ceasing to be, that is, with death.

The world was perceived as hostile and challenging, in which every day there seemed to be the need to fight to stay alive a while longer, until the last day arrived in which the fight would no longer make sense and finally the battle for survival would be lost, since everything comes to an end. Faced with such a perceived reality, the mind was stunned. It felt that it had come to a combat field and saw no other options. The deafening noises of perceived warfare had prevented it from looking beyond the seemingly obvious to the sweet, serene face of Christ, in whose reality it happily dwelt forever. So it was for many millennia until it was ready to glimpse—to remember—that there was something beyond what the eyes saw or bodily senses perceived.

II. To the Light of the Father

As the memory of truth began to dawn in universal consciousness, humanity—and with it the rest of the physical universe—began to rise. Its mind and heart, along with every aspect of creation, began to live consciously united with Heaven. It was no longer a humanity that only fought to cling to life in the exhausting battle for survival and the supremacy of the "fittest." Instead, it began to remember its divine origin, and that this origin, although nameless, was perfect love. It was ready to receive Christ in its own flesh. Not only did God begin to remember Himself, but with that memory He became one with everything created, as He has always been. It ceased to be a remembrance, becoming one with everything and everyone in a close, direct, real, integral reality.

When Christ manifested as a man, a new creation arose. Or rather, his incarnation became the source of the new creation. A new reality springs from it, which began to manifest immediately after that "universal consciousness event" manifested in form. By becoming one with a human body, the creative power of Christ was set in motion through his divine spirit to create the new Heaven and the new Earth, the convergence of God's holy creation. Naturally, this concerns not only the physical aspect, but also the mind, heart, soul, and everything part of human reality, as well as the material universal.

Perhaps the question still exists in your mind as to why the human soul was given the option of following a path of the opposite of love that would entail pain and suffering. For what purpose would such a path be created, even if it finally led to the bliss of divine knowledge and perpetual happiness? To understand, it is necessary to be sufficiently stripped of ideas of the learning mind, and go to the memory that dwells in the center of being—a remembrance so ancient that time cannot embrace it.

Be silent inside. Close your eyes if necessary. Allow the sweet memory of your Divine Mother to shine with greater luminescence in your holy mind. Let the softness of truth show itself to you joyfully without judgments, preconceived ideas, or interpretations. Just be silent, watch, and remember.

In that memory of the moment of the creation of the idea of separation, you will recognize that it is not that the soul was given a choice among many, which would include some that cause damage, suffering, and lack of love. None of those things are an option in God or in you. Love does not propose destructive things, nor the truth foolish things. The option for separation was not, as such, an option. It was an effect of the desire to create a reality of self-awareness apart from union with the whole. It is a way of creation of the soul not in harmony with the creative Source.

III. The Urge to Be

The soul never creates anything contrary to love. What happens is that when she decides to create in her own way, without remaining united to her Source, she manufactures things the effects of which, due to her ignorance, she does not know. Does hearing this—or living it—come as a surprise? Or are you surprised by what happens so often that surprise seems to be a natural aspect of existence? Do you not decide things that you think will be a blessing, and they are not? How much pain is created by not being aware of the consequences of actions!

The soul did not want to suffer. It was not receiving a punishment for sin. Give up those beliefs forever, for they will prevent you from living fully in the consciousness of resurrection.

Rather, the soul sought a unique identity with separation. But it tried to achieve this without involving its Source. It is as if it had said: "I want to know myself. For this I will create an identity that allows me to be unique, unrepeatable, and also knowable. I myself will determine what I am." This stemmed from the notion that no one could know itself more than itself—the germ of egoism, a consequential state in which the soul is its own source of knowledge and action.

The soul knew that God is infinite mercy, but did not know what that consisted of. Therefore, the idea of being her own creator, in the sense of defining for herself what she is, did not engender fear or rejection, since she knew that her Divine Mother would if necessary correct that creation together with her. The audacity to create in the manner of a soul separated from God is not so great if one understands that the knowledge of the soul included the knowledge that whatever it created could be re-signified in love and reunited with truth. Have no doubt that this knowledge is part of you from all eternity.

You know that you are not alone, that you will always be loved, that Heaven exists, and that it is your home. You know this very well. You also know the infinite goodness of the One who not only created you, but also sustains you in existence with Her infinite sweetness and eternal holiness.

When you chose separation, you also saw that Christ would incarnate, and that the resurrection would recreate everything in holiness and justice. You also knew that walking this path would have you reach a degree of union with love that no other path would achieve. That, also, was an effect of your choice. You saw, you observed, and you chose the perfect path to become like God in God, which is the will of your soul and that of your Divine Mother.

In your own way you created an authentic universe of experiences. Every aspect of that creation was brought together in

Christ so that, while continuing to honor your creations, they may be benevolent, harmless, holy, and filled with the true beauty of your being, just as you have always wanted. In other words, everything you created and believed in will always be respected and loved. And if it is not grounded in the truth, my divine love will gently take it into my hands, show it to you, and together we will re-signify it, bring it to the throne of light, where everything given to love is sanctified because of what the child of God is.

7.

Emissaries of the Resurrection

I. The Portal to Eternal Life

C hild of the Most High, if someone climbs the world's highest mountain peaks, does he seek an accident or death? Of course not. And yet it often happens that expeditions, even those undertaken with great enthusiasm and much preparation, end in pain. What happened?

I am not using the example of mountaineering to judge that activity but to generalize the truth concerning all activities of the soul. The soul sometimes acts without thinking about possible consequences. Is this caused by an insufficiency or disability? No, it is simply the free choice of not wanting to know, creating a state of willful ignorance.

It would not seem very sensible that a soul, created by God and full of His divine light and goodness, can choose an option that brings about suffering due to not being aware of the consequences of its actions.

Before embarking on the path of the world, that is, before experiencing the phenomenal world of time, space, and matter, the soul knew everything it needed to know—the totality of what that option meant. And it chose out of love. It knew it would have to experience the absence of God, the aridity of a desert in which it would not remember its divine Source with clarity. It also knew it would see things that love would never create. It also always knew that divine mercy would express itself in an eloquent and graceful way. It knew that Divine Mother would be with it, even in this world.

The soul always had the knowledge, and always will, that pain need not distance it from God or from its true being. It also knows perfectly well that the access door to resurrection, to return to the Father's house, would be located precisely where the paths of the world intersect. It knew before entering, that at some point on the Earthly path she would answer the question that her Divine Mother asks her in every moment, saying sweetly: "My daughter, give me your soul."

When the soul born of holiness was ready, she would have the certainty of responding in perfect freedom. This would not be another simple answer, but would arise from the deep knowledge that love is what she herself is, and that her happiness, joy, and fulfillment is only in perfect love. Through the ways of the world she would come to know her Source, where her home resides and where sweetness dwells. That is why she goes through it all—because she knows the ways of the world have the ability to take her to the heart of God, which is where she longs to be forever.

II. The Message of the Resurrection

Part of the thinking mind wonders why I speak of separation, guilt, and its effects, especially after knowing that this has already been transcended. After all, whoever receives these words has chosen love and left the ego behind, along with the countless non-loving complexities. I shall answer.

I bring up the matter of separation here so you can see it in relation to the whole, which will cause an unprecedented transformation in you and in the universal consciousness of which you are a luminous part. Until very recently, schools of thought, including theology, philosophy, and spirituality, not to mention systems of government, have centered on a belief in the essential evilness of man, the mystery of sin, and how to deal with its effects. This has been done in countless ways. You know it well.

I have said that we are no longer in the age of reason, but in the Age of the Heart. This means that from now on, the resurrection is what will occupy the central place of consciousness. Indeed, you have come into the world to be its apostle. Everyone who hears the call of love and follows it is invited. Nobody was ever asked to be an emissary of guilt.

"I have not come to judge but to save," I said when I walked the paths of the Earth. I came and I continue to come through those who listen to my voice and follow it, bearing witness to truth. Therefore, my message has been, and always will be, that of resurrection.

In order to achieve resurrection consciousness for everyone, to make it visible and available, I went through the redemptive passion. But stopping there without looking at the whole, and not focusing on the goal, is to miss the point. It is to not understand that the means were simply that, means, and never ends. The end is, will be, and always has been, the resurrection.

I did not come into the world to perform miracles *per se*, nor to indoctrinate, nor to reveal a dormant knowledge. None of those were my purpose. I came to open the doors of resurrection. This was well understood by the first messengers, often called apostles or disciples. But with the passage of time much has been forgotten, and the collective mind focused on pain, and with it, guilt. Nevertheless, that was part of the path of the evolution of consciousness, or if you prefer, the journey of creation to the resurrection. It is simply part of the past, not the goal of the soul.

III. The New Creation

This work comes to open the floodgates of hearts and consciousness to begin a new era in humanity, and with it in all creation: the consciousness of resurrection. My beloved, I am revealing to you your role on Earth, just as it is in Heaven.

What else can Heaven be but the resurrection itself made an eternal and conscious reality? I came to give you and all creation eternal life. That is the treasure that the resurrection brings to you who receive these words and to everyone who has made the option for love, or makes it in due time according to the designs of the soul and God.

Telling happy stories was a request I made to begin to break the habit of spreading fear, pain, and other things that grip the human heart through words and memory, a custom so ingrained in humanity that it is difficult to think of living without it. And yet, from this point on we cannot go on with the thought pattern that shares hopelessness and fear. This new path—new and eternal at the same time—sets aside everything that does not come from love. The new Heaven and new Earth is the perfect expression of resurrection consciousness. It is its effect, the conclusion or consummation of divine creation.

If you take away the vision of the truth of resurrection, you lose sight of the whole. Such a concept of reality cannot come from divine knowledge because reality is universal totality. One of the great drawbacks you have had up to now, as an individual and as a human family, has been not integrating the resurrection into your vital understanding or worldview. If we look at things simply, as is always the case when looking through the eyes of love, it will be easy to understand.

The soul is created by love. She is then called to deliberately choose to live in the truth, that is, to participate in divine glory, which is not only its Source but also its inheritance and its natural habitat. Just as when birds were created, they were given a firmament where they could spread their wings and fly freely. Fish were given the waters of streams, lagoons, rivers, and seas so they could swim and manifest themselves according to their nature. Likewise, the Kingdom of Heaven was created for the pure soul. Only in the Kingdom of Love can the soul unfold its potentiality, because of what it is.

8.

Energy of Pure Truth

I. The Flow of Beautiful Love

Sincere joy is always justified because the resurrection is the ultimate reality of being. What is being revealed here, or rather what we are being reminded of, is that if but a part of the evolution of things is considered to be the totality, truth is lost sight of. It also brings to mind the fact that the works of God cannot be understood while they are being carried out.

That is what has happened in human understanding up to this moment when a new portal of light opens, and through which truth begins to flow in a magnitude of holiness never before experienced on Earth. Nothing can stop the transformative force of the energy of pure truth flowing from the heart of the Divine Mother to every aspect of creation.

Living in resurrection is living centered in the reality of Christ, and therefore in truth, because the new Heaven and the new Earth is the only divine reality, the blessed effect of love in all things. It is the Omega born of the Alpha, the end that gathers within itself all origin. Have you thought that God's plan would end in guilt? Such or similar thinking is very typical of the ego, for in guilt consciousness the ego is God, which engenders fear.

But to continue such a belief is unnecessary, since it is simply not true.

Beliefs can change, as you know. Still, they remain beliefs. You are not now being asked to believe in a new doctrine, nor to replace a structure of apparent truths with others equally illusory. No, for you know very well what is being revealed. You know who is speaking. You hear my voice calling you to life in every moment. You know very well that I am the resurrected, and that time, matter, or space cannot limit me. Therefore, I can speak to your heart in countless ways—and not only you who receive these words, but everyone and everything. There is no limit to my being, just as there is no limit to you.

What this work comes to give the world cannot be known through the intellect or the effort of learning. Although I use some words directed to the mind and others to the heart, the power behind them is understood and accepted by conscious-ness. Truly, truly I tell you, beloved of Heaven, humanity is ready to accept resurrection consciousness as the ultimate reality of being, as the goal of its way of seeing, thinking, and living.

Guilt is a temporary, limited state of consciousness that precedes the resurrection. Therefore, it is part of the path but not the goal. It is an experience, among many others, that carries within itself the potential to join me in the resurrection. Have you not already done so? Of course you have, otherwise you would not be here, listening to my voice with all the love in your heart.

Is it not true that your soul sings, resonates, and trembles when hearing my voice? How could it be otherwise, if the voice you hear is that of your Divine Mother in you, being your own and only true voice? Remember, beloved, the light that never goes out is the only language you can understand, the language of love, which speaks in the voice of holiness.

II. Levels of Existence

The resurrection was a universal fact of consciousness, and an eternal fact. In this lies your definitive escape from guilt and from everything not in harmony with your being. You may argue that guilt was also a universal fact of consciousness, insofar as it encompassed all aspects of creation. But that is not necessarily true.

Guilt is not an act of consciousness but a denial of it. That is why we can accurately call it unconsciousness. And since it is a negation, it cannot have power or substance. This is the same as saying it is not real. You have to understand guilt as the effect of the denial of love that the soul experiences, not in the totality of its being but in a minuscule part of it.

Accordingly, it follows that guilt is not only not an act of consciousness, since it is its negation, but it is also not universal since it does not affect the totality of what the soul is. Thus, there will always exist in you that luminous, healthy, pure, holy, and wise part that nothing can sully or touch.

The world can be as it wants, and so can your life experiences. You can even plunge into the deepest darkness if you wish. Nevertheless, that radiant part, full of light and beauty and imbued with divine knowledge, will always shine in all its glory and continue to create a new holy love in union with the Source of endless life. This you know very well. That is why, despite everything, you feel deep in your heart that hope is always justified. How could it not be if you know the Heaven in which your being dwells forever in unity with everything that is holy, beautiful, and perfect?

Remember, love regenerates; fear degenerates, therefore what the experience of the opposite of God causes is instantly undone. It has no substance. It lacks a nucleus to sustain its existence because the Source of life comes only from the center of the divine heart. What is not aligned with it simply cannot exist.

III. The Gifts of Love

What will happen to all the untrue thoughts and unloving feelings that you seem to harbor in your heart? They will just vanish forever. They were there for a while as an experience on the human journey. But at the journey's end, the angels will breathe on the souls and all of it will go away, never to return. And the truth will remain shining as always. Only from that moment will it be recognized, accepted, and embraced by the totality of the soul, without any part hiding from the light. Will this be love's gift because you merited it? Of course not.

Let me now address this question of effort and merit, a very ingrained belief in the world's thought system and one that constitutes an obstacle for the mind that wants to live in peace. Believing that universal chaos has been created because you attacked God's creation and by your merit will be undone, allowing you to return to a state of Grace, has been adhered to in many areas, practically all.

Observe how the idea that we have just expressed leaves love out completely. It would seem that the soul, by itself, had the ability to change creation and also the power to restore it. Why was the separated mind capable of conceiving the idea that it could restore what had previously degenerated? Because it knows that God can have all things be reborn from the spirit. This is the same as saying that love makes all things new. In short, the soul knows resurrection.

We could say that the problem resides in the fact that the separated mind, being identified with the ego, attributes to itself God's prerogative to do and undo. Why is this a problem? It is in the sense that the separated mind believes something illusory. Then she convinced herself that her fantasies were real, and was left in a state of ignorance of reality. Going a step further into that nonsense, she intended to use that same ability to create illusions to solve the problem that she herself created.

How could the cause of a problem be its solution? If so, either the problem never existed, as happens in the tricks of illusionists, or the solution exists since it comes from something not its cause. And so it is.

While the separated mind uses thoughts as if they were magic wands to create illusory scenes, love awakens that part of the soul that was dazzled by illusory tricks and brings it back to the reality in which it has always been living. She does so out of love and volitional acceptance of being. In other words, the soul does not wish to live apart from God, and therefore it returns. Always return to your first love to restore yourself in God.

9.

The Kingdom of Unity

I. The Power to Create

My daughter, my son, sun of my sun, you need to remember that the new world is already here. It is one full of goodness, harmony, holiness, and perfect creative power. Its appearance resembles the old world, although in almost nothing that is meaningful. The forms do not remember what was once the nightmare of separation. The forms are so united to the formlessness of God from whence they come that they cause only joy, serenity, and peace. In other words, the new reality, which manifests the perfect unity of Heaven and Earth, carries within itself everything you wanted to create from your heart but without a single glimpse of what made you suffer.

The new creation is as benevolent as your being, as holy as you are, as divine as Christ. In her the eternal and temporal, spirit and form, divine and human are perfectly united. To a certain extent the world you are currently perceiving with the body's eyes and grasping with the intellectual or reasoning mind, is one in which nothing totally fits with divine vision, even though your creative power seems to manifest in it.

The new world is as human as it is divine, just as creation in the mind of God has always been. There is no reason why what you are as a human should be removed from creation. It just needs to be redirected into the light of your true spirit. We can say, without straying too far from the truth, that the current phenomenological world that the separated mind feels is its home—although less and less—is something like a blank slate onto which you have been trying to create in a manner so alien to your true creative power that everything is out of place from what you really want and what you are.

In the old world you were created to survive. In the new, you are created for the simple reason of being. In it you are aware that your spirit constantly creates in unity with Christ, creating a new holy love. Remember, light of my eyes, that love creates only love, and that only love creates. The rest—all those forms of creation in the world to which you have given attention and that you have often admired—are a pale glimmer of your true creative power.

In the new world, and only in it, the power to create that resides at the core of your being is fully released. The creative flow manifests unceasingly from God Himself to you and from you to everything. In the new world, and only in it, your relationship with the divine creative power is never denied.

The thinking mind may argue that when I walked the Earth, I demonstrated that there was no limit to my power, which I showed through visible and eloquent miracles. Even so, I assure you, blessed soul, that that power was hardly the slightest hint of the power of God in you. Since it has no opposite, words cannot explain it for it is unrelated to what the current world calls power.

Your power is one with your glory. You do not yet see it perfectly, but you have had glimpses. The divine power resides in its entirety in your heart. It is so serene that it only spreads peace, so pure that it only creates purity, so subtle that it is like an almost silent whisper that creates beauty. Nobody sees it, hears it, or even feels it; but all those who live in the consciousness of the resurrection—which is another way of describing the new Heaven and the new Earth—see its effects and are aware of its magnificence.

II. A Journey to Truth

If form is the expression of the formless, if manifestation is the expression of the unmanifested, then we can say that the new Earthly Kingdom is the union of divine consciousness, which is beyond all form, and its perfect manifestation, including you. All this occurs without any distortion or interference—God's plan come true.

What else was fear but a denial of your true power? You have already experienced that fear not only degenerates but limits, even to the point of paralysis. Fear reduces mental abilities, including the capacity to discern. If you let yourself be carried away by fear, it will to a degree block the expression of the soul's powers.

That is true, however, only in the realm of illusions, in the phenomenological world. In Heaven, the only reality created by God, none of it is true because what you are cannot be limited. This eternal truth is what you live in the new creation, towards which the physical universe is moving more and more rapidly.

Everything not coming from love imposes a limitation and enslaves the soul in some manner. You have experienced this, but it occurs only in the pseudo-creation that you call life as you conceive of it from that side of the veil. But on this side, where everything is seen with the eyes of Christ and is understood with the mind of God, none of that is real for the simple reason that it is not part of divine creation. It may be part of the continuum of the soul's journey, but that does not make it real. I will clarify this.

As has been said, creation travels from the moment of its call into existence—its birth from the womb of the Divine Mother—to the point of the option for love. From there it goes to the stage of awareness of the Christ within and then enters the state of consciousness of the resurrection and into the new creation. In this sense there are stages, not in eternity but in the consciousness of time.

The four stages explained above constitute the journey carried out in every aspect of creation. None of them are accomplished without the presence of God. However, there is one stage, that of Adam's dream, in which the soul can deny its existence and to a degree forget its source. That does not mean that divine love is absent nor does it make the soul any less. But it does cause your soul to stop seeing the glory of God directly. That stage includes the time that the soul takes between its creation, when it hears Divine Mother ask, "Will you give me your soul?" and its realization of the fundamental option for love. This stage is a matter between each soul and its Source.

III. Love that Sanctifies

Fully fearful awareness resulted in the denial of your true power. Although one not in harmony with your being, it was an available option, since despite everything, you have the power to create. You cannot lose that ability. At most, all you can do is confine it to a world of fantasy where your pseudo-creation has no direct relationship with God, is limited, and destined to disappear. When something becomes increasingly limited, it eventually disintegrates. That is what the stage of ego identification consisted of: an experience marked by a lack of integrity.

Love gathers within itself all things and sanctifies them because of what it is. In their perfect union lies their power. Remember, what is not united cannot be powerful, for power and unity are one and the same.

As I said two thousand years ago, a kingdom divided falls. That is what happens with the realm of time when it is not linked to eternity. That is what happens with the kingdom of the ego: It succumbs due to its impotence, which means that it cannot be creative at all. Nothing coming from it can create. Only God can create, which is the same as saying that you can only create in love.

Can you begin to see why the option for separation was made? Can you now understand that it is nothing more than an illusory state in which the mind pretends to be distant from its Source and from everything coming from its divine being? Can you glimpse that all this has been done in order to experience Her absence, to finally realize that the only thing that makes for happiness is to live in union with the Creator Mother? Do you now see how everything makes sense, even though you may not fully like the option you chose?

Just as the soul enters the world of separation, or illusion, through forgetfulness of Heaven, it also enters the new creation through forgetfulness of separation. In other words, the forgetfulness of being, which is a state of amnesia of the true identity of the soul, is replaced by the memory of its true being in Christ. Once it makes that reversal, which is in itself the resurrection, the new world stands radiant, luminous, and perfect in the eyes of Spirit. Spiritual vision is revived. The mind and heart are awakened to truth. With this, the power of love, which constitutes the reality of what you are and is a power so holy and so great that it gives life to everything that exists, is claimed forever.

10.

Song of Resurrection

I. Always New Melodies

The effect of resurrection consciousness is the new Earthly Kingdom, where everything is joy because everything is love. This bliss is not like that which comes from things of the world, not even like that reached in the highest ecstasies of contemplation. No, not even the highest mystical experience that can be had in the old world can compare with the joy of the soul that dwells in eternal truth. It lives on Earth where the sun never sets, and whose light is so soft, and at the same time brilliant, that it caresses souls while giving life to everything. This light never wanes. It emanates colors of unspeakable beauty.

There, my love, in that Kingdom that has always been given you and which you will soon enter, sounds become shapes and shapes become colors. Movements engender songs whose melodies make the heart resound and sing. Everything is beauty, joy, vibrant vitality, and perfect strength. You will speak with the angels, not like in the dual world experience where they whisper words of eternal life into your soul, but rather you will speak with them face-to-face. They will be for you what they have always been—dear friends whom you have known forever and who know you like the back of their own hands.

Beloved humanity, men and women all, sisters and brothers in Christ love, these words are addressed to each one of you:

those of you who are in time; those who are gone; those who will return to choose again; and those who will dwell forever in the new Earthly Kingdom. That is, they are for all creation.

Truly, truly I tell you, to think that the world is moving towards or living in a dystopian state is to misunderstand. Humanity, and with it all creation, is moving faster and faster towards the achievement of the times of plenitude of love and from there it will make its triumphant entry into the new land, which holiness has created and prepared for everyone forever.

Are the new Heaven and the new Earth like Eden was? Is it the lost paradise re-found? No. What was described as the Garden of Eden in certain cultural contexts is the state of consciousness prior to the path towards the fundamental option. The degree of knowledge of God that the soul had in that state cannot even be compared to what you have now, or with the one reached in the temporary state of denial of being, much less in that of the new creation.

Movement to a greater knowledge of God's love is in itself the path of the soul, of all souls, and is not exclusive to human beings but in common with every aspect of creation. It has been said in many currents of thought that there are various states or degrees of consciousness, each of which carries a kingdom. As an effect of this, the idea of the current Earthly Kingdom, or world, was conceived, as well as the Kingdom of Heaven, which is understood as having levels or degrees. This led to the idea of hell and other dimensions, all of them explained by a vertical line, locating God in the heights and the opposite of holiness at the bottom. This was a way of explaining things.

II. Everything is Unity

You no longer need believe in various levels or realms of God. How could the divine reality be sectioned or divided into disconnected realms? Everything is united in love or it would not exist. Even so, the degree of union with love is a matter of free will and this in turn corresponds to the nature of each aspect of creation. The Kingdom of the Resurrection is not a place or a dimension of creation reserved for some. It is the destiny of the soul, the purpose for which it was created.

You may believe that the God-created soul has become entangled in the web of ignorance of the ego's thought system, as if it were a tiny insect caught in a spider's web. But my beloved, you who receive these words, that is not true. What was trapped in a world of illusions was simply a thought from the mind of the soul. Just one. It may seem like a myriad of thoughts, a swarm of ideas, but truly I tell you that the thoughts you think you think are only a thought of separation. Just one. They may come in various forms, but still, they are one.

There is only one thought, and that is the pure divine thought. Nothing that is not that thought can be considered as such. Therefore, you cannot think many things. Indeed, the real mind does not think anything. The idea of a mental course is so foreign to the divine mind that it is inconceivable in the new Heaven and the new Earth.

The unified mind, totally integrated with Christ and therefore receiving the only all-encompassing thought that comes from God, is the only thing shining in the soul that consciously dwells in the new creation. To a certain extent we can say that the thought of resurrection is the perfect expression of the pure thought of God in sonship.

Just as in the past the state of guilt constituted the central axis of the thinking mind, the knowledge of resurrection will be the sign of the new times until it can be fully lived. Beginning with it now for you is the primary purpose of this revelation.

It is not possible to explain in words all of what it means in the new Heaven and new Earth. Nor is that the central intention of this work. What we seek here is to anchor your memory, and with it that of all creation, in the reality to which the soul is called and towards which the entire universe is heading.

There is music in Heaven as there is also on Earth, but that of the new Earthly Kingdom will be a trustworthy expression of divine music. Mankind could not have conceived of the idea of music if there were no music in the heart of God. Remember, the ego only distorts things; it never creates anything because the ego is devoid of meaning and therefore of substance. Only the essential can create music because all creation comes from the Source of beautiful love, which is where the creative power of the Divine Mother dwells, and from where everything that exists emerges in holiness.

When resurrection consciousness dawns radiantly in your mind and heart, that is, when it is embraced by your humanity, not only is the body glorified but also everything that constitutes your humanity. You become a new humanity, not simply as pure potentiality but as a conscious reality; not as something unmanifested, but as a manifested, resurrected being.

Divine music unites in love. That is its function, just like everything that is part of the new creation. It is not like mundane melodies, but reminds you of melodies in Heaven. When a single note emanated from the heart of God, a universe of infinite universes of love was created in unity with you. Each one of them carries within itself that note, which will vibrate and be sung as part of the eternal song of creation. It is an endless hymn of beauty and joy that has no comparison. Each of them, so to speak, carries within itself all the power and glory of God.

It is music that not only makes the heart happy, but also creates life through its sounding.

III. The Glory of the Resurrection

The music of God is perfect knowledge. Its melodies, whose beauty is indescribable and whose joy causes a contemplative ecstasy in the soul, spread wisdom throughout all creation. Naturally, this cannot yet be fully explained, since it is only understood in the language of consciousness, which being the language of love has no words. Still, I am telling you that you have already remembered this music.

You delved into divine melodies and their ineffable reality every time you were at peace. You have also done so during every moment of prayer in which you joined Christ, and in every act of holy love you gave to the world. You have savored its beauty whenever you felt a heavenly presence while walking serenely through a park, or when entering the silence of a forest. You have heard these melodies in your soul when contemplating a sunrise with your heart in your hand, and when, looking into the eyes of a newborn child, you jumped for joy remembering the purity and innocence that you seemed to have lost, but which are yours forever.

My beloved, I want to give you the memory of the new Heaven, which is one with the new Earth, where your home is forever. I ask you to close your eyes for a moment and let the remembrance of Christ's resurrection, and with it yours, spread in you.

Holy son, out of love I invite you to make the resurrection the only source of your knowledge and action. Behold it. Meditate on it. Immerse yourself in its silent reality, so austere and subtle that the world has practically forgotten it. Still, you and

I are here to remind everyone that we are the resurrected, that the resurrection is the destiny of creation, and that its reality is now, always.

Daughters and sons of truth, listen with loving attention to this: The prayer that once said, "Our Father who art in Heaven, your kingdom come" will now be:

Being of my being, Source of endless life, grant us the grace of the resurrection shining in us. May the knowledge of the new Heaven and the new Earth shine in all consciousnesses, now and always. Amen.

Make this prayer yours that I give you out of love and you will be joining the consciousness of the resurrection. By doing so, you gather in it all humanity, thus allowing love to be the only Source of knowing and acting, because together we are the resurrection and the life. We are the light that illuminates souls and the life-giving truth. Be glad that it is so.

11.

Beyond the Christ In You

I. Everything Converges in God

It may be that the world seems to be in chaos, that humanity is degrading in many ways, and that nature has somehow joined in, expressing disharmony in various aspects, all of which creates a real sense of lack of peace and fullness. This can be what the mind observes and what the heart contemplates that has not accepted the resurrection. Indeed, this vision of what surrounds you is perceived as so real that it may be hard to imagine that the world will finally live in the peace of God. And yet it will be so.

So you ask yourself with sweetness and love: Must we wait for that moment to arrive? Must we continue to walk under a scorching sun, in an inclement desert, thirsty for love and truth, and continue to experience the absence of peace and holiness in a world that seems submerged in madness?

I invite you, pure soul, to stay for a few moments with those questions. Observe your feelings, the reactions of the body. Perhaps the mind prepares for fight and defense, and the body tenses up, or maybe not. But keep watching still, quietly waiting, full of gratitude to the love of loves.

Once you have plunged into the fathomless abyss of your consciousness, take these questions and, placing them before its luminous throne, you will remember the truth. You know, not by intellectual reasoning, but by divine knowledge, that the answer is "no." You know that the new Earthly Kingdom and its union with the new Heaven are within you, as much as Christ and all the true creation of God of which you are a beautiful and irreplaceable part.

If you allow your imagination to be embraced by the wisdom of divine love, what is said here will be shown to you clearly, not because you cannot understand it or need external help, but because you but honor who you are when you allow divine Spirit to deposit the knowledge of truth in your mind. That part of you that we call "elevated" or "the divine Spirit in you" is your being, your true identity. The rest is an illusion that has long since ceased to exist.

II. The Rest of the Soul

Living centered on your "I Am" and from there moving towards what cannot be described or defined because it is beyond all limits, is where these words are taking you. You have already identified with Christ. It brought a transformation to your human experience without precedent and of a magnitude that surpasses the imagination. But this is not the final goal of the soul. You need not stop there.

Perhaps your soul's journey seemed long, winding, and often tiring, so much so that you feel the need to say: "I have arrived. I don't want to travel any more. I just want to rest in the peace of my divine beloved. Let me be cradled in the arms of my Divine Mother!" You yearn to be immensely happy in the truth.

Make yourself one with that feeling. If you could release everything else and allow that emotional state to embrace you, you would feel a gentle yet powerful hand lift you to the heights of the heavens of your holy mind.

Truly, truly I tell you, beloved of my divine being, that what we are doing here, and the transmutation of identification with Christ towards the I Am, will not require even the slightest effort on your part. It is not something you need to achieve or do. It is simply the blessed gift of your Divine Mother for you who receive these words, and for everyone who has identified with Christ-love.

What is happening in your soul through these dialogues is that you become aware of the true being that you are beyond even the Christ in you. Perhaps you think that this contradicts what has been said previously in which I said over and over again that you are already the realized one, that there is no more distance to go, that you have found your true self, and there are no more searches. And all of that is true, for I am the truth, the way and the life, as you are.

Why then need we go beyond identification with the Christ in you, towards the I Am in God? What does that statement mean? It means that I love you with a redemptive love, as you already know. We cannot allow your mind, so inclined to constant chatter, and to re-configure reality in its own way or make associations of what you believe to be Christ, distancing you from the truth.

III. From Love They Come, To Love They Will Return

The path traveled up to now which has been carried out through words, a loving expression of universal consciousness which we have called a movement of beautiful love, has served the purpose of disengaging your mind and heart from the idea that there is separation—a lack of integration—in your being. This allows what you really are to begin to shine in its divine glory, like the holy love that constitutes the foundation of your being.

The transmutation of human nature has already been accomplished. You are now a new humanity, and not just you, but everyone—one ready to be swept up in the sweet energy of truth already pouring from the heart of God to you and the entire universe.

Remember, when I visibly showed the resurrection on Earth two millennia ago as counted in time, with the purpose that some may be living witnesses of that event of universal consciousness and share it with others, I told them: "Do not touch me, because I have not yet ascended to my Father." And I also said, forty days later, that "I am going to prepare the heavenly mansion in which each would dwell eternally in endless bliss and the infinite beauty of holy love." I said this with other words but with the same meaning being remembered here.

What is being said, son and daughter of holiness, is that once you join the resurrection consciousness, that is, when you accept that you are the resurrected because I am the resurrection and the life, the path of ascension of your humanity begins. You are no longer the incarnated Christ who brings to the world the knowledge of truth, bearing witness to it in love, but your human form rises in such a way that your glorified body and your ever-holy spirit become one eternally. You return to the state of light in which bodies and spirits exist in perfect harmony.

Listen, my daughter, to what your Divine Mother has to say. Receive it with docility, peace, and sincere joy. These words contain within themselves the knowledge of the purpose of your existence and that of the entire universe. This revealed truth, here remembered, will be the cornerstone on which the building of the thought system of the new Heaven and the new Earth will be erected. Nothing can knock it down, because that firm rock is God Himself.

I offer the following to say to yourself, and if your mind wishes, to give your heart the joy of living every day in the ever-true truth, the indescribable joy that comes from certainty about the purpose of life, and the guarantee of your return to love. You may make this expression a prayer, or a mantra if you prefer to call it that, or a litany, to make the power of wisdom of your words recreate your humanity in the holiness and eternal novelty of what you really are. I tell you, beloved child of my divine heart: *From the Mother you have emerged, into the world you have gone, and to the Mother you return forever in love.*

Rest in my peace!

12.

Love Is Everything

I. In the Mind of Christ

Beloved son and daughter of holiness, a new humanity is being born. However, this must be seen in the light of the wisdom of Heaven, so that old thought patterns do not do what they used to do—interpret things based on learning from the past, not anchored in truth.

To believe that the new, emerging humanity will be a new "type" of humanity that does not include every human being past, present, and to come, is to continue to believe in separation. To think like that is not to think at all, since that way of apparent reasoning does not come from the mind of Christ, which is the only Source of true knowledge and is eternally united with love.

That perfect union is the foundation of the new Earth and everything that inhabits it. The new Earthly Kingdom is an expression of souls in the new resurrection consciousness, totally united to Christ. Spirits that wish to manifest themselves in it do so for the length of time they arrange. This is the only point it has in common with what we could call the old Earthly world. Everything else differs completely, since it is a loving extension.

You are as much a part of the new humanity as every human soul. In the new Heaven and the new Earth, the light of Christ is shared with the beauty of all divine creation, all living things.

That some express themselves through physical forms and others do not, and still others do so only from glorified bodies in spirit and truth, does not create any separation. Consider the analogy of music.

Musicians include everyone capable of creating music that involves rhythms, melodies, duration and sequences, all of which finally leads to the consummation of the various types of musical works that they create.

The fact that some musicians express themselves in a particular genre does not make them more or less than those who manifest in another. Every musician is a musician regardless of how his or her artistic ability manifests. Something similar happens with the new Earthly Kingdom being revealed here. All are artists of love creating a new holy love in perfect union with the Source of endless life, each soul in its own way.

Only pure souls full of love arrive at the new Earthly Kingdom, and they arrive for the purpose of spreading love in a particular way. They are Christed souls totally united to God. In God the divine and human are perfectly expressed in unity. This applies not only to humans as you know them today, but to every aspect of creation. The plants will not have poison, nor the animals the impulse to prey or use poison to defend themselves. Nothing will hurt anyone, or be hurt.

II. In Love There Is No Vanity

The thought of heartbreak, or lack of love, is not part of the new creation. Nor will it be necessary to fight to survive, because the new Earth will feed everyone, and the new air, too. For those pure souls that remain eternally united to the creative Source, their food is love. They need nothing else. What bodies receive will for them be the perfect expression of the love of creation.

You may wonder now, what will happen to my soul if it has already come to the Earthly plane? Will I also dwell on the new Earth? In order to answer this essential question it is necessary to remember that in God's creation nothing happens randomly or in vain. Therefore, your passage through the Earthly expression is not by happenstance.

The glorified bodies or resurrected souls—those who inhabit the state of full consciousness of the resurrection among whom you are—do not need to live in the more condensed physical plane, even in the new Earthly realm. You know and experience that your union with all souls is perfect and you remain in holy communion.

The veil that now exists between the physical and spiritual does not remain in the new creation. Therefore, you will be as united to Earth as your Divine Mother is right now, and as attached to Heaven as she is. The interaction established between one and the other will not be ruled by current laws. No distance between Heaven and Earth will be experienced, just as Christ does not experience a distance. You will see everything through the eyes of God and experience everything through His divine heart.

Having said the above, it is important to understand that in the new Earthly Kingdom, which is linked to the new Heaven, free expression of love is perfectly consummated. This means that there will be souls that will temporarily manifest in the physical plane and others that will not. But all, without exception, remain united in their entirety. There is no forgetting of God who has brought so many souls to a world of beginnings and endings in which the laws of love were not perfectly manifested, with the sole purpose of remembering.

III. Communion and Resurrection

The new Earthly Kingdom is governed by the laws of Heaven. This is why you need not express yourself again in the realm of time even if it is loving: one life; a single identity; a single temporary experience; one holy being.

The pure expression of the soul leaving the current Earthly experience is spiritual, but not in the sense that it lacks form, but that the form is a divine expression of love, which is its reality. There is no need to abolish form. I have spoken of this throughout the various works that have been given.

When I say that once you leave the realm of time as you currently perceive it, but live in a spiritual reality including holy or glorified forms, I also mean that you are not disconnected from anyone or anything. In effect, you re-connect with everyone and everything in total and perfect union. This is what we call "communion." You are never more aware of each loved one, of each living being, and of each aspect of creation, than when you complete your cycle back to the Father's house, back to love.

Communion, to be such, must be reciprocal. It cannot be one-way. Therefore, in the new plane of consciousness called the new Earthly Realm, not only do you see and know all beings perfectly, but they know and love you perfectly, without interference. Simply put, you consciously stand in the truth that you are not alone, never were, never will be, and that there is no loss, ever. You know vividly that lack and limitation are inconceivable.

Naturally, my beloved son and daughter, we are trying to put into words what is beyond words. Even so, your mind has risen high enough as an individual and universal family to comprehend, even in mental language, what is revealed here.

We are no longer at the stage where words are an obstacle to accessing the truth, since they pointed elsewhere, or because the separated mind dwells on what is literal or has limited meaning.

Now your humanity is placed entirely at the service of love. Therefore, we can express in symbols what is beyond limitation. We can do so because the distance between the symbol and what it represents no longer exists. Now, being and expression are united. We remember that there is much more beyond words.

We know this since the light of truth shines in all its glory in our holy mind, so we can go beyond words toward the truth they represent. We also know that the reality of the new Heaven and the new Earth is far vaster than what can be expressed here. But that does not prevent the symbols we use in this revelation from illuminating memory and leading us to remember God and the knowledge of the most blessed gift of his endless Mercy: a world full of peace and love, a new creation whose foundation is truth—Christ.

Stay silent, my love. Let these words fall on your mind and heart like dewdrops that water the beautiful garden of your soul and allow the herbs of perfect knowledge and the blessed flowers of holiness to sprout. Stay there, next to me who am your beloved and divine lover. And let us enjoy together the memory of love that has no beginning or end and which gives us all a new Heaven and a new Earth where we will dwell united forever in the joy of the children of God.

13.

Memory of the Resurrection

I. The Flight of Being

Beloveds of holiness, son and daughter of the supreme good, I have to reveal, or rather, remind you of a sweet truth, since the knowledge shared here from the Heaven of the One Mind dwells in you as well as in everything. The loving truth I refer to is the eternal fact that the convergence of creation is the resurrection.

When you were created as a most pure, holy extension, full of the beauty of perfect love, the history of your soul was also created, since in creation everything happens at once. There is no time in eternity, at least as you conceive of it. Therefore, the creation outside time of your soul reality includes the instant of creative light, that moment in which you were called into existence, in union with your will to be. Within it was the option to exercise free will through separation, or identification with the opposite of love, in order for you to consciously choose Christ. And there was also the resurrection along with it where dwelt the existence of a new creation: what we here call the new Heaven and the new Earth.

After remembering that the resurrection, as a reality of divine creation, has always existed in the mind of Christ and is the point of convergence of the journey of creation, it only remains for us to remember this: Love makes all things new, that is, whatever it extends to is renewed in its essence and reality.

When love extended to what the soul had created without love, that entire dimension of existence was transmuted; the Divine Spirit banished from it everything that was totally opposite to truth, and sanctified that which was in harmony with it, either totally or partially. In this way, He restored everything that needed to be restored, causing the beauty of the soul to shine brilliantly.

Imagine the world of illusion, the realm of separation and guilt, as a creation that, when you called it into existence, had dissonant elements, like music with discordant notes. Then love "adjusted" it so that it would not only be the creation you really longed for, in total harmony with God's will which is also yours, but that it would be a living expression of the beauty that are you.

The creations that the sons and daughters of God create without love can and should be restored by love. They can be, because love has the power to make all things new, that is, to adopt every form and embellish it because of its embrace of light. It must do so because you never wanted to suffer, nor did you want to live forever in a world devoid of meaning. Therefore, your Divine Mother, who sees into you secretly, always knew that your will was to live eternally in bliss. Although perhaps your creations did not reflect this perfectly, at the center of each one of them is a spark of holiness because you are its creator and a child of holiness.

II. With the Eyes of Christ

Everything that comes from you, be it a thought, a feeling, an action or omission, whatever it is, carries within itself the seed of perfect love. Just as a musician can create a piece of music and then tweak and change it, something similar has happened with your creations, with the difference that love does not spiritually recycle, nor does it adjust or restore itself. Rather, love renews everything in holiness. Only God can do that, and does. You know this well because you have experienced the transmutation of your humanity into the new being that you are. You know that you have stopped being what once you were, and became new. And not only that, you are new in every moment, because love is eternally creating.

If the resurrection is the convergence of creation, and I assure you this is eternally true, then we can conceive of its history as an evolution of consciousness. Strictly speaking, there is no such thing as evolution, because what comes from God is perfect and complete, just like you and all creation. However, for the purposes of understanding with the thinking mind, we can say that there is an evolution in the sense that what was asleep begins to awaken. In other words, the soul begins to come out of the state of amnesia of being and begins to remember who it is, where it came from, and where it is going.

The awakening of consciousness to truth is actually a reconnection of the soul with being. Or if you prefer, reconnection of the mind with spirit. That is the only union that needs to take place, since the separation is simply a thought far from truth, although one that has created a particular experience, as all thought is powerful and creates form on some level.

Since the only level in which the mind can create something far from God is in fantasies, it is there where the experience you call guilt or illusion is lived. Even so, within it you create loving things, because love is never absent from you.

What you really are will be with you forever, and wherever you go I will go with you. We cannot be separated because I am what you are; you are the being of my being. You know this even if you still don't live it fully.

The resurrection state of consciousness which we are remembering here is the cause of your existence and the joy of your being. In that consciousness is the eternal unity of holiness, the Source of who you are and therefore of your uniqueness. Therefore, you can see with the eyes of Christ, think with the Mind of God, and create in union with your Divine Mother, the only Source of true creation.

III. The Lasting Joy

If your mind thinks of God and nothing but God, if your heart beats in tune with the spirit of holy love, if your body is a member of the body of Christ, what else could you experience but eternal life in all its length, width, and breadth? Can you begin to see what your resurrection consists of? Have you already seen how your Divine Mother, who is also the Mother of all creation, never leaves anything unfinished, since she is the Source of meaning?

What is incomplete lacks purpose because it has not reached its conclusion, its consummation. It cannot be part of true creation because God is the perfect completion of truth. In other words, love does not abandon the work of its hands. She would never let her children cause harm to themselves, even though their creations, albeit illusory, can create a painful existence.

I'll put it another way. Can you create something without love? Yes, although only in a world of illusion, for such a creation, or pseudo-creation, could never enter the realm of perfect love. Still, if you believe it to be real, you need to be saved from that belief in the sense that your mind needs to be corrected and reintegrated into true creative power. The reintegrated mind rises to eternal life.

Since the resurrection comes from Christ and illusions from nothing, the exchange that takes place when resurrected is simply the recognition of fear as the nothing that it is, and of love as the everything that has always been, is now and always will be. Love is recognized as what it really is, along with the absolute insubstantiality of everything created without love. This recognition—not with the intellectual mind but rather as an awareness—is in itself the resurrection consciousness in which you truly live forever.

Once the light of resurrection illuminates the entirety of your mind, you return to Heaven just as Jesus did. No one not in that state of consciousness can go with you, since they are not yet ready. However, once you rise to the holy abodes, you are indeed united with everything and you can see them as closely as if you and they were walking together hand-in-hand.

Does walking a path with a blind sister mean that you cannot see her as well as care for her, embraced in loving mutuality? You are never separated from the love you have given or received, even in the illusory world. All love is holy and eternal because of what it is.

Do not think that the love you have felt in the old world has been fruitless, or that your charity has fallen on deaf ears, or that the acts or feelings of compassion that you have given to the world have stopped creating loving effects, or that your prayers have stopped reaching the heart of God. It has all had the power to bring Heaven to Earth.

Remember, beloved of my heart, nothing can stop the power of love, not even a childish fantasy, however powerful and terrifying it may seem. Truly I tell you that the creation of the new Heaven and the new Earth has been carried out in perfect unity with you who receive these words in union with the entire universe.

14.

Being Resurrected

I. A Remembered Voice

Holy son and daughter of love, light that extends from the heart of God, today I come to talk to you for the good of your soul and that of many others. I come wrapped in divine glory, which is as much yours as it is mine, because it is what we really are. Let her embrace you and give you the warmth of a love without beginning or end. Allow me to spend some time alone in loving intimacy with you. Open your heart and mind to receive this revelation from Heaven.

Beloved of the sun and stars, of the wind and everlasting spirit, beloved forever in Heaven and Earth who come from the Divine Mother, I come in a joy that derives from spreading the light of truth about the resurrection. I do this to remind you that you are the resurrected. Therefore, your reality is beyond all limits.

When I rose in the humanity of Jesus of Nazareth, you rose with me. And not only you, but all of creation. The reality of the resurrection is a convergence of perfect love and eternal life. It is what you are.

You were not created to be temporary—not you, nor anyone or anything. Everything that comes from my Divine Maternity is eternal, because of what I am. The experience of separation or of unconsciousness is a limited option that souls could go through, but which—as I have already said—would trigger the resurrection. There are seven stages of the journey of all creation: creation, invitation of love, separation, election, salvation, return to unity, and resurrection. In each phase there is free will.

If you are the risen one, just as I am and as is every brother and sister who receives these words or has reached this point on the path, why do you not feel the joy of eternal life? Why does the world seem more immersed in guilt than in resurrection? Because the journey of creation has phases. Each of them has a state of consciousness from which you can access the other sphere. They are all interconnected since everything is unity.

In the state of guilt there is an access point, or portal of light, to the consciousness of the choice for love. This is why duality allows you to go beyond that plane to the power to choose. Indeed, that power is itself the portal of light mentioned above.

II. Portal of Holiness

In the state of separation or guilt, there is a door that leads to what we call the fundamental option, which is linked to what we will call the total salvation of the soul. In fact, these states are like concentric circles, similar to those that you can see in a serene lake after throwing a pebble into it.

We are more precise if we replace the words "door" or "portal" by that of "path" or "bridge," because once the soul in its Earthly experience makes the fundamental choice for love, total liberation from all that is contrary to truth results, reaching salvation, while remaining in the freedom of the sons and daughters of God.

Once the soul has freed itself from all ties—which is done perfectly upon the crucifixion of guilt not carried out on a cross but by making the fundamental option for love—it returns to conscious unity. The world of options fades in its awareness. It begins to live in a reality that has no opposite, that is, in the truth. Dissociation has been transcended. Separation has been left behind. After that, inevitably, the resurrection consciousness occurs. In it, everything Earthly human is reconfigured and transformed into a divinized humanity.

The journey of consciousness, as explained in this dialogue full of love, is not something your soul does alone. All of creation takes the same journey in unison. The difference between journeys is that each phase can be carried out with more or less time associated with it.

The separated mind completes each stage of its path in the time it determines. Even so, since psychological time, the time created by the separated mind, is illusory, the decision to linger in time has no real impact on the being but only in the experience of that small part of the mind that believes it can be separated from love.

Beloved of my divine heart, do you realize that each phase mentioned here is a state that can be attained? The resurrection is the state in which the pure soul, and all of its powers, remains united in God, that is, in perfect love. In resurrection consciousness the mind thinks what Christ thinks and the heart feels what love feels. But since Christ is love, what really happens is that the totality of the soul lives surrendered to divine love, or if you prefer, to holiness.

III. The Gathering of Heaven

If thoughts and feelings are a unit, and each triggers its counterpart in the other, then when you feel what love feels, and think what truth thinks, then everything else will be its living expression. You may be wondering how to achieve this. Let us remember the answer together.

The being that you really are does not undergo changes of any kind. It does not need to be resurrected or saved. Salvation is for the united mind and heart—indeed, it consists of both united, vehicles of spirit, always integrated, always one.

It is not possible for the mind and heart to stop being a unit, since each feeling triggers a thought and this in turn triggers a feeling. The relationship between the two is always undivided. Even so, the mind can disagree with the heart and the heart with the mind, creating the state of conflict, or separation. Achieving reconciliation between both aspects of the soul is what the state of unity or salvation means.

In order to pass from one state of being to another, it is necessary to reconfigure the mind and heart. If the soul tries to do that by itself, it will remain stuck in the same state of guilt that it created with its way of thinking and feeling, because only the being can create a state of being, not the soul.

In the context of this dialogue, we call "soul" the human identity that makes you the human being you are. In the case of an animal, the soul is that part of its being that gives the animal its unique animal identity. "Being" has no attributes. The soul gives identity to each aspect of creation; therefore it has attributes or powers, namely, the mind, the will, and the understanding.

Continuing with the clarification of terms that we are sharing here, thoughts and feelings reside in the mind, which are usually associated with the bodily aspect called head and heart respectively, although in reality both are manifested in every fiber of the body. The body is an expression of the mind, or the garden where it deposits the flowers and herbs of the soul's experience. We make this clarification so that the thinking mind does not get lost in definitions and to be able to continue our heart-to-heart dialogues, walking together on a clear path, under a clear sky full of light and peace.

15.

The State of Grace

I. Words of Eternal Life

When I inhabited the Earth in the humanity of Jesus, I who am who I Am not only showed the way to the resurrection but also made it a conscious reality for the universe of time, space, and matter. Remember, I said that I was the way. In doing so I not only pointed out the path to the fullness of being—that is, the resurrection—but I created it, for in me there is no distance between saying and doing, between my will and its realization.

What is being remembered here, beloved of divinity, is that the plan of reconciliation, the reunion of the human with the divine, has always included respect and integration of everything on the material plane of existence. By this, I mean that the way back to love, back to truth, would be—and indeed is— one in which the laws of time would be placed at the service of the truth. Nothing in the physical universe has been or will be destroyed by God. There is no reason for that.

Love has the power to make all things new. Therefore the temporal plane can be renewed through the divine embrace of love. And that is what happened while also respecting the original need of the sons and daughters of God to have time for their return. Time is used, so to speak, for the purpose of guaranteeing their serene arrival at the house of the Mother, thus reaching the state of Being in Christ. This is why you experience your resurrection in successive phases. To be more precise, it is not your true self that experiences sequences or stages, but that part of the mind that created psychological time to experience separation. Everything else of you lives eternally in the resurrection.

Time will collapse. Actually, this is what we call the achievement of the new Earthly Kingdom or the end of time. There is no proper "end"; in creation there are no endings, since God is eternal, infinite reality. However, the mind created a state in which it sees from a temporal perspective, in which it seems that everything is born in one moment of time and ceases to be in another. But none of that is true.

II. The Unity of the Resurrection

What is born and then dies is not real. It is simply an illusion, something like a movie where a story is created that has a beginning and then ends. Or if you prefer, an empty canvas, created by the separated mind, where it paints and unpaints figures. This is how the son of God entertains himself, building sandcastles on the seashore, all of which vanish after being hit by the waves that come from the ocean of my divine love, or by the wind that stirs up the breath of my spirit. All this happens until the soul—in union with its divine Source—determines that endings are no longer only for all the things projected in that false reality, but for the experience of separation itself.

The time from the separation experience to the return to full resurrection consciousness is something each soul has arranged in perfect harmony with its holy Source. When you made that choice, you knew that you would return, and that the resurrection would be Divine Mother's gift to you whom she loves with a love without beginning or end, with a love so great that it surpasses all understanding of the thinking mind. This happened not only in your human singularity, but in collective, universal human nature.

In creation, all is unity. Therefore, when humanity was submerged in separation consciousness, every aspect of reality—each person—was also submerged. That is what the myth of Adam and Eve tries to describe, representing all humanity as a whole and also each part of it.

In the story of the so-called "fall" described in Genesis in the Bible, it is said that the woman and her offspring will crush the head of the serpent, a symbol that represents the universal separated mind. What was meant? They wanted to express clearly what is revealed in this work: that ultimately, a woman, the feminine aspect of God, would bring about the restoration of the state of separation.

The "woman and her offspring" refers to me, your Divine Mother speaking to you now, as well as to you and all my daughters and sons united in the fullness of love. It refers directly to the time of Mary, the time of the entire history of creation, which recently is manifested in a more evident way.

In the very instant that the mind created the state of non-being—the consciousness of separation—creation was given to divine motherhood in a new form. Creation had always been hers, because everything belongs to love, but a new dimension of the feminine aspect of God was set in motion: the birth of Christ in separated humanity, which would open the portal of consciousness of resurrection, opening the floodgates of the universe deified in its entirety.

III. Resurrect in Me, Now

Daughter, son of the light that always shines! Can you begin to see how great is the mercy of God? Can you understand why hope is always justified? And also endless joy? Is it possible for you to understand now to a greater degree why discouragement has no place in truth? You have already risen—not just you, but all of creation, and not because of your merit or effort, but for the simple reason of love. So big is the heart of this Divine Mother who has created you in the infinite joy of truth! She knows that your true being rests in Her arms, always loving Her.

Here is a question that I invite you to return to: Why has humanity focused so much on the guilty, condemnatory aspects of history, despite the fact that from the beginning it has been shown that the resurrection and eternal life would be the convergence of creation, anticipating the sovereignty of the heavenly Mother over all creation? The answer is in what you believe. And since humanity's beliefs bear witness to what their will yearns for, we can say that the will to be special and live apart from love has kept the mind trapped in the experience of a reality that, although illusory, engenders suffering.

Once you have answered the question of who you really are, you put aside the state of separation and return inexorably and immutably to the state of grace. This happens when in the depth of your heart you decide to drop the defenses against love and truth; consequently, you immerse yourself in the experience of Christification. That is, you resurrect.

How you choose to express your resurrection is a matter of your uniqueness. Not everyone expresses it the same way. This has also been demonstrated in Jesus and Mary, who each expressed the resurrection differently. Jesus demonstrated that his being—both human and divine—is unlimited, therefore nothing and no one can hinder his glorious body or his holy spirit. Mary, the Assumption of God, expressed in her glorious elevation that death does not exist and that the dimension of Earthly limitation is far from the end of the road. She is the ever-living, ever-pure, eternally illuminated. She is the woman whose offspring heal the separated mind and elevate it to the mind of Christ, whose humanness becomes full in God.

To you who receive these words, I say lovingly, if you have said yes to love and have decided to live in the truth—which I assure you that you have already done because you have made the fundamental choice, otherwise you would not be here—you live now in the resurrection. In other words, you are resurrected.

16.

Eternal Light

I. Universal Light

Graceful soul, the difficulties that you often experience living here and now in a conscious way like the resurrected person you really are, reside in a misunderstanding. You believe that the resurrection is an act, a particular fact, an event, since the world has understood it that way. This presumes that the event has nothing to do with your identity or your present consciousness.

The resurrection has been understood as something that happened to a single specific man who was raised to eternal life to show that perhaps you, and many others, or even perhaps all some day in an uncertain future, may experience the same thing. That is the same as believing that Heaven is ahead in time, in a moment separate from now, and that you must cry out for it or wait for it. Such an idea perpetrates separation.

The itself event occurred on the material and temporal plane in the lands around Jerusalem. But as you already know, that was the visible aspect of something invisible. It is a form that perfectly represents the content, with no distance between the symbol and what it symbolizes. By understanding things from this perspective, you can begin to glimpse the fact that the resurrection was not an event only but a new state of being that the entire physical Universe, or realm of time, entered.

The resurrection is total or not at all, because in Christ every-thing is integrated in perfect unity. By accessing the state of resurrection consciousness, the part of creation that had fallen asleep or was submerged in the dream of separation, was rein-tegrated into love. In other words, the fall, or state of denial of truth, was terminated.

Why was the manifestation of resurrection to eternal life expressed at that particular moment, rather than before or after? This is due, beloved of my divine heart, to the fact that the consciousness of the filiation, in particular the separate aspect of love from it, opened to receive me. I am the light of the world, as I said. And that is true, just as you are. Even so, that light that illuminates consciousness, which is the vital force of truth, could not fully enter a heart that would not accept it freely.

At the moment in which the consciousness of the created was by its own choice ready and willing to receive me, then my divine power responded and entered it. Christ entered the dream of Adam, and from its union with it, resignified everything in love. It caused the soul to return to the House of Truth. This is not to say that the spark of divinity that exists in every aspect of creation had not been shining at the center of everyone and everything before what has been called the First Coming.

When truth entered the house of fear, everything in it became light. Individual consciousnesses began to see. The will of each aspect of creation began to move, heading towards the sun of the true being that each one is. That is, it was directed to the recognition of its true identity, which it shares with everything in Christ. As a result, everything that was dispersed inside and outside the soul was re-unified in love. All duality was tran-scended. All polarity was abandoned.

II. The Gift of Eternity

The resurrection not only proved that death does not exist, it also testified that the Earthly world as you know it now, with its dimension of time, is not even remotely the only reality. Life does not end on Earth. In fact, it never ends. What power can whatever lacks life have over life itself whose reality is God? Demonstrating that there is no power that can attack love, nor any force that can even touch it, since only love is real and the rest is pure illusion, is what was evidenced in our resurrection.

Observe, my son and daughter, that I said "our." I did so deliberately. From now on I ask you not to think of my resurrection as an individual and separate fact. Along the path of awakening to truth and love, which we have undertaken together, I have asked you to abandon many beliefs that distanced you from unity, and you have. One of them was the belief that I am superior to you, or separate from what you are. Many other similar ideas were already transcended into holiness. Now I ask you to accept that you are resurrected, since I am.

To accept that your Divine Mother, for the simple reason of love, resurrected you even without your being fully conscious in your present humanity, is simply to recognize the truth. You are not a sinful soul who trembles as you fearfully walk the roads of the world, waiting to see if you are lucky enough, or given grace, that your Creator will let you into Heaven when the day comes to leave Earth. You are the eternal expression of divine love made human. You are life-giving light; holiness with a human face. You cannot die because I am the God of the living, the Mother of truth and love. I am as eternal as you are.

As you already know, the thinking mind is the servant of spirit. All it does is bring you to the place of present consciousness, the experience that justifies what you seek to reaffirm. And this is always a question of identity. Remember, every thought system is founded on the cornerstone of what you think you are. A soul that fervently believes it is separate from God will create a building of thoughts based on that faith, and her mind will show her that she is right, even if it is not true. Ask the mind to show you the truth. It will. Ask it for anything else, and it will do it for you too.

III. The Resurrected of Love

Remembering this powerful revelation about how the thinking mind operates, we begin to allow the truth about the resurrection to be received. And we joyfully say:

I am the light of life. I am the joy of the resurrection. I am eternal. Death has no power over me because I am eternity. I am, because Christ lives in me, just as I live in him forever. I am eternal because I am the child of love and truth.

Repeat this prayer filled with the power of Heaven to yourself as many times as you feel the need to do so. Each word will water the mind, bringing forth new life, new thoughts so similar to the truth that they will illuminate the world and the entire universe. And your soul will joyfully sing a hymn of praise and gratitude as it remembers the beauty of your being.

Truly, truly I tell you that each word expressed in that prayer given here out of love is a drop of wisdom from the Heaven of truth towards the beauty of your holy humanity. They all come from your divine spirit, which is the only truth about who you are.

Be glad to receive this, because in it resides the memory of the resurrection that is already alive in you. You begin to let go of all the limitations that the learning mind has created in a past that seems close, but is now so far removed that its distance cannot be measured in terms of space or time.

I assure you, beloved of my being, that the experience of separation—the phase of denial of the truth or of life that never was, all of which we call the past—is much more distant from here than east is from west. Everything has been fulfilled.

Today is a day of immense joy, a time of happiness and peace. A soul has arrived at the Father's House. A daughter of God has recognized the truth. She has accepted for herself the resurrection as the blessed gift that her Divine Mother has given for the simple reason of love.

Now we close our eyes to the world, we put aside all belief, all brooding of the mind, all interpretation. We let go of the desire to understand things as formerly understood. We renounce, at least for a moment, our old way of seeing. This is how we make an empty space within ourselves. And we plunge in unity into the sacred silence of our heart. There, in the depth of the soul, we listen with happy astonishment to the angels of Heaven singing to the love of loves an everlasting song full of beauty and harmony. Their hymn says to you, very specifically to you: *Blessed are you, the risen with love.*

17.

The Law of Life

I. Human and Divine

Beloved soul full of grace, I am Archangel Raphael. By the blessing of Divine Will, I am given the gift of being the bearer of this revelation manifested in this dialogue of love and truth. As you already know and have experienced, there is only one true voice which is that of Christ, king of kings, love of all love, light of all true light.

My archangelic heart sings to the greatness of the lord of life and Creator of all that is holy, perfect, and pure. With Her divine power She extends love eternally. Her divine motherhood creates abundant life in a constant flow that nothing and no one can stop. The infinite becomes form in love. One of those expressions, which nevertheless gathers within itself the essence of God, is you who receive these words. Blessed heart, you have been chosen in the design to co-create together the new Heaven and the new Earth.

Light of resurrection, holy thought, being of perfect love, you are the joy of creation. I know that you still cannot experience in all its dimensions how much happiness is extended to the universe due to your existence, but the day will come when you will be aware of it, and the humility that comes from living in truth will melt you into an everlasting song of perfect praise and deep gratitude. You will see the glory of Christ spreading from you everywhere like a mighty river of light—divine grace manifesting from the center of your heart to everything and everyone.

The rays of divine reality that emanate from your being embrace everything. They are the extension of the embrace of love. Nothing is excluded from them. Soul in love, you who have risen to eternal life in the unity of Christ, you who have made the fundamental option for love, I tell you that the light of all true light which no eye can look at without being blinded, pours out all over your being and embraces all of what you are. And from your holy reality, you yourself extend it to the rest of creation in unity with your sisters and brothers, with me, and with the Mother of love.

The perfect union of human and divine is itself the resurrection because it is the convergence of form with the content of truth. It is the expression of love and its Source, the joy of sharing as it is in God. Do you listen in the center of your heart, to how the flowers sing and to how the birds dance to the rhythm of the wind? Her song and dance are her unique way of expressing the joy of existence.

There is no more sublime expression of gratitude than a sincere smile of the heart which lives joyfully in love. This is how the hearts of the sonship abide forever in the perfect reality of God—among them is you, the unique form of Christ in you. Truly, truly I tell you that without you, our Divine Mother would lack something. She would be incomplete, not in her essence, but in the knowledge of creation. You were created as a holy expression of the will of perfect love to make itself known. This you know well.

II. Only Life Is True

Despite the fact that your mind is the bearer of the truth revealed here, you have not yet made eternal life your only way of thinking, feeling, and being. This is what—in truth and not in illusions—it means to live as the resurrected that you are. If death does not exist or have consequences, and if endless life is the only real thing because it is the only true thing, what room can there be for sorrow? Where could sadness dwell? What sense can there be in battles and guilt?

Beloved sons and daughters of the world, please listen to what I come to remind you of by the grace of the loving will of the Divine Mother. You will not die. Nobody will die. Nothing that has been called into existence will cease to be. I assure you that the stars will remain for all eternity, as will the stones and the wind, the planets and daybreak, bodies and spirits, minds and music.

Everything to which Divine Mother gives life is eternal because of what She is. This is the immutable law on which life rests. Nothing can change it. If well understood, you will know that the laws of love, of nature, and of cause and effect reside upon it. She is Herself the Source, the origin and the end of all true law. Even those that govern the dynamics of atoms and elements are subject to Her, along with what moves the soul and mind, spirit and heart.

There is life beyond time. There is love beyond the Earthly experience. There is God's will in Heaven. There is discernment and everything you are capable of conceiving or not conceiving. There is no possibility that you could vanish into nothingness, nor that your mind, your soul, or anything in the universe cease to be what it is. This is why the inexorability of the resurrection is perfectly acceptable. Without it, eternal life would not be eternal.

My love, as you know, many children cry when they are born. This is due, among other reasons to their fear of separating themselves from the state in which they were, and having to transit into the Earthly experience. The opposite happens at the moment of the "definitive embrace of love"—the name that I sweetly ask you to use for the transit made from the realm of time to that of no-time, towards the true life you live eternally in God.

Daughters and sons of holiness, how often have you heard that death does not exist? That there is only life without end, infinite joy, an eternity of love? Even those who with a sincere heart would answer "never" or "rarely" carry within them the perfect knowledge that eternal life is the only reality in which everyone remains forever united with God.

Consequently, whether you have heard that statement often or not at all, you know the truth of it. You came into the world with holy knowledge, a foundation of all truth. Nevertheless, you have not yet made it the cornerstone of your thinking, feeling, and living.

This manifestation of Heaven given here for the good of many is given to you so that, from now on, you make the conscious choice to support your entire system of thought, feeling, faith, and hope, in the perfect certainty of your resurrection. Not as something that will happen, but as what you are and therefore as your reality now and always. Blessed soul, you who receive these words, remember that you are the resurrected, which is the same as saying that you are love and nothing but love.

III. Resurrection Is Eternal

Beloveds from all over the world, if after walking together the path of beautiful love in union with Jesus, Mary, the blessed angels of light and all the true creation of the Mother. and with all the revelations given through this blessed pencil in the hands of love, you are still waiting for the resurrection to be the final prize, you have not advanced far enough.

To live forever in the arms of love is your destiny. You cannot comprehend this with your thinking mind. The goal of this work is not to substitute one thought system for another. In fact, those who have reached this point on the path know it is no longer necessary to think about anything or to apply mental effort of any kind. The truth we are remembering here is well known by your being—the knowledge of the love of God and of what you are.

Never before has the resurrection been so directly associated with the true identity of being. Herein lies the central grace of this demonstration in which, thanks to the healing of memory you have already achieved, you begin to accept the fact that you are the resurrection and the life. This shift of consciousness is of such magnitude that you cannot imagine its universal effects.

Is it not true that to abandon forever the idea of death is to loosen the fundamental stone of the world's thought system and the foundation of separation? Does this not mean putting aside the cause of all fear? That is how radical is the call that love makes. Love asks you to stop merely believing in the resurrection so you can move on to be its trustworthy expression, its pure manifestation. That is why I remind you now, over and over again:

Graceful soul, born of the Mother of eternal life and sustained forever in her divine love, the Source of all creation, you are the resurrection and the life. You are one with the truth.

You who receive these words, I invite you to repeat them to yourself, out loud if you prefer. You will be accompanied by truth, your mind will rest in peace, and your heart will rejoice because it will recognize the truth in this voice of love.

Blessed are you who have opened your humanity to receive the grace of holiness from Heaven!

18.

The Joy of Resurrection

I. Love In Freedom

Sons and daughters of God, you have been searching for truth and have found it, even in a world that seems to have denied it. You received the gift of this revelation by the grace of divine will and your own. You seek to love as Christ loves, and think that you have not achieved it yet.

I have said that you are called to live in the joy of resurrection. This is not a new commandment, nor an imposition, but an invitation. If accepted, happiness without opposite and a peace that encompasses all of God's creation will flower.

You have been told in the various revelations received, of which this is an integral part, that everything exists within the embrace of love, and that a house of cards—for that is what the guilty state is—was erected within the universe of truth. You are reminded of this so you understand that resurrection is the bridge that unites the Kingdom of Heaven with all states foreign to love. Without it you could not escape the illusory state of guilt.

Any state of consciousness that the son or daughter of God wants to create without love must be allowed, although it must also have an escape, a way to return to divine consciousness. I will clarify this important matter but first remind you how much I love you, how precious you are to my divine being, how full of beauty, grace, and goodness you are, soul of my soul, being of my being.

Beloved of my heart, allow me to reveal something about creations that do not have their foundation in the divine will, that is, in perfect love. When something like that occurs, it is because of what the soul believes to be its right to create in a way different from God's way, as free will demands.

When the soul fabricated for itself the state of guilt, or separation, it made a choice. Love respects everyone's decisions. This is why it allows the soul to create dimensions alien to its divine reality. This is not an irresponsible respect for the freedom of God's children, like a father allowing his very young son to fly a passenger plane. Rather, it is because he knows that there will be a "vortex," a "bridge," or "channel" that will allow him to return to the Father's House, to the virgin soul as it was created. In short, love knows that it will never be separated from the soul, nor she from him.

I said before that every state of consciousness foreign to divine will, foreign to love, carries within itself what allows it to be abandoned, so the soul can always return to truth. The resurrection is what embraces in the sanctity of the divine being everything that does not proceed from love, and transmutes it into a state of perfect unity with Christ. Then what was dispersed is reunited, what had been lost is found, and what had been denied precisely because of its truth is once again recognized as the foundation of everything in God.

II. In the Abodes of Heaven

There is one consideration of great importance that needs remembrance here. Although it is true that any foreign state of consciousness can be abandoned forever to the divine will and the return to Heaven accomplished, it is also true that the reverse path cannot be made. You who are the resurrected of love, know that you cannot go back. One cannot go backwards in consciousness, for once reached, a degree of consciousness is never lost.

Perhaps somewhere in your mind you hear the following question: If all that is true, how is it possible that the soul ever fell? What can guarantee it will not happen again?

This question is the result of a deeply rooted thought pattern in the thinking mind, one that we must put aside forever since it belongs to the old world, which is not here. What fell was never the consciousness that you are. Your being remains forever in the Heaven of holy love. What happened is that the mind began to believe a childish fantasy as if it were true, and then fabricated a false reality.

Can you forever abandon a false belief in the reality of an illusion? Of course you can, because of your will to live in truth. Remember, my love, that believing in fantasies is not a property of consciousness but a minuscule aspect of the mind.

No one is resurrected to die again. If so, it would not be a true resurrection. You may wonder then: Why were there some who were resurrected by me in the time when I testified to truth in the form of Jesus, who later tasted death? That is because, beloved of my heart, the leap of consciousness from true resurrection to eternal life had not yet occurred. That jump happened a little later in time, after my death on the cross. Until then, no one could experience the resurrection state perfectly because the mind of the son of God was not ready to accept it. But finally it was. First, the ego had to be abandoned on the cross in order to transcend it and reunite everything with Christ. Did I not say: "Father, why have you forsaken me?"

It is evident that the abandonment of which I spoke could not refer to that of my being. What love abandoned was not me, who am its reality, but what many call ego, or false identity. Abandoning it, the ego vanished forever for it had no meaning; it dissipated because of its own insubstantiality.

III. Love Never Leaves

Is it not true, beloved soul, that you have sometimes felt as if God abandoned you? Let me tell you what that means in the light of love. When the ego withdraws from the soul that was identified with it, it feels as if its own being is leaving, or as if it is passing through the death of its identity. In a certain sense that is real, since after believing that you are what you are not, when you put aside the false self, you feel that you are the one who is vanishing. This sense of loss of self persists until the beauty of the Christ who you truly are begins to shine forth in your heart. In other words, until Christ rises in you, reborn into the love that you truly are.

Can you realize the absolute impossibility of being abandoned by love? What dies, never lived. What ceases to be, never was. In this truth lies your escape from the world of illusion, birth, death, and from the whole world.

I never let myself be carried away by illusions. I always knew the truth. I walked the roads of the world being fully aware of that knowledge. The same happens with you. Perhaps you have believed that for some years of your Earthly life this knowledge was veiled from your consciousness, or that you did not have the ability to live in harmony with that divine knowledge, but to think like that is to keep thinking about an unreal, untrue past. Remember, the past is meaningless. There is no point in looking there for answers only the truth can reveal, which is the eternal presence of God.

When I said that my Father had abandoned me, I wanted to testify to my perfect and total union with all creation's experience of suffering. I know, because I know every beat of your heart and that everyone experiences a sense of being abandoned by God before their enlightenment or union with Christ. This happens not only on an individual level, but also collectively. Indeed, it is what the world is experiencing now.

God has not died, nor will He ever die, for He is eternal life. However, what does die is the identification with the false god that would replace love—what we call the ego, or the illusion of your identity, not because it has a name but so that you can distance yourself from its insignificance and release the false belief that it is what you are.

Naturally, for a being who believes it is what it is not, when its false self is brought before the light of truth to be seen for what it is and then abandoned, what usually happens is that it believes that it was God who abandoned it, despite the fact that it is actually the mind that always abandons what is not true and never was true. When that happens, the light of Christ shines again in all its glory in that small part of the mind that had denied love as the only Source of its reality. In other words, once the choice to abandon illusion is made, the soul is resurrected to eternal life.

19.

United in the Resurrection

I. I Looked and Saw You

Soul loved by the whole universe, once again I tell you, you are the resurrected of love. Note that I have not said you are resurrected or that you have risen, but that you are the risen. This is because your being and the resurrection are one. You could not be resurrected if resurrection wasn't an aspect of who you are, and not just you, but the whole universe. Just as you can return to love because love is what you really are, in the same way you rise to eternal life because you are the resurrection and the life.

What is being brought to collective consciousness here, to the universal mind, is that in the center of the heart of every living being, regardless of its form, is a spark of eternal life which constitutes its only reality. In it resides the infinite power of perfect love, which includes every holy virtue, every beauty, every truth manifested and yet to manifest, as well as the resurrection to eternal life as one of the treasures of the Kingdom.

The time in which you are living, daughter or son of eternal light, is the temporary space that exists between the event of your resurrection and that of your glorious ascension to Heaven. This path, which is experienced as if it has phases, is the one that the entire universe travels, individually and collectively. I was the first to walk and show that path. I did so in the figure of Jesus. Remember, being the first does not mean being the only one; it simply means that others will follow me, you being among them.

When I was resurrected, or more precisely, when I opened the door of resurrection consciousness for the universe, I saw your resurrection next to mine. I looked at you from the glory of my being and saw you shine forever in the ineffable beauty that you are. I looked and saw you. Yes, you—very specifically you who receive this revelation now. Remember, there is no "everyone" to whom I speak. "Everyone" is a concept. I speak to you, and I do it heart-to-heart. You know where these words come from and you know they are true.

In the center of your heart is the knowledge of your resurrection in union with mine. We speak as if we were two separate beings so that this can be understood by the thinking mind, but in truth there is no distance between one and the other. We are united.

II. Yours Is the Resurrection and the Life

Truly, truly I tell you, there is no such thing as "my" resurrection or "your" resurrection. What exists in truth and not in illusion is a totally loving consciousness that gathers within itself all that exists, sustaining it eternally in a life that never ceases and a bliss that never diminishes. That consciousness is God Himself, perfect Love. It is the Source of creation—who you are.

If Christ rose, you too must have risen with him, in him, and through him. You know, since you are already well grounded in truth, that the resurrection cannot have been for God, nor exclusive to His incarnation in human form. That would make no sense. Can what is eternal resurrect? Hopefully not.

What was resurrected was that small part of the mind of the son of life which had denied eternity as his only reality. In order for this to be possible, he extended to the plane of form the redemptive power of Christ, the capacity of love to make all things new, bringing them back and sustaining them in the state of grace.

If Christ lives, you also live, for you are nothing other than the Christ in you. How many times do you remember or think about my resurrection? Infrequently, right? Can you see how little room is in your thought system, and in the world's, for resurrection? I have already spoken of this, but I return to it here to look at it in a new light.

If there is a belief deeply installed in the thought structure of the world, it is the reality of death. Whether you realize it or not, the faith that death is real is the cause of practically everything the world does or does not do. All fear finds its root in death, as well as all lack of love. There is not a single thought of the ego not oriented to the belief in the inexorability of death.

It may be that various spiritual paths teach of eternal life and a Heaven, regardless of its name or the attributes ascribed to it. Nevertheless, the belief in Earthly death as real remains installed in the mind and heart of humanity as a primary pattern of thought. Transmuting this is the purpose of this revelation.

It is of little use to recognize this truth if you do not make it the point of convergence of your mind, your heart, and everything that you are. Knowing that there is no such thing as death, that it cannot come from God and therefore it has no foundation, no substance, or reality, and yet to continue living as if you did not know it, is foolish. That would be to know what you are and live as if you were something else.

III. A New Holy Being

The resurrection is the gift that, as your Divine Mother, I have always given to you and to everyone, for the simple reason of love. It did not happen in time, but at the very moment of your creation, since it is part of who you are. What happened in time is the awareness of it, or its manifestation on the plane of form or consciousness of separation. What is manifested comes from the unmanifested. Therefore, there must be in you a center whose divine power extends resurrection.

To resurrect means to call back to life what died, what had ceased to be. We could say that it is to revive, to be reborn, or to "be again." Isn't that what already happened when I created something new out of you, and you left behind the cloud of amnesia that made it difficult to see and accept your true being and which made you believe that you were what you never were nor will be? You know that you no longer live but it is Christ who lives in you. And that you have been reborn from above. You know that you are a new being. What you have not yet accepted is that therein lies the resurrection.

Ask yourself: What is it in you that one day ceased to be, and then needed to be embraced and revived by the power of resurrection? The answer is obvious: everything not real. This is because all that you are is holy, eternal, and unchanging in God. And yet I rose again. How is this to be understood? It is understood when you remember that the resurrection is the embrace of love which extends towards illusions and dissolves them forever, leaving in the soul only that which is true, the pure extension of Christ, the essence and being of all creation.

Energy that emanated from love—"resurrection power"—transmuted everything it touched, causing that which was dissonant with the loving will of God to be recreated into perfect communion with Her. Remember, truth has no parts into which it can be divided. Although we use different expressions such as divine will, perfect love, or resurrection power, they all refer to the same thing. They speak of that which is the Source of all being, of all life.

My love, where does your knowledge of the resurrection reside but in your longing to be? In that irresistible force of being who you really are beyond all contradiction? That desire to be, even where it seems to be diminished to almost nothing, contains within it all the power of God, including the power to give new life to all things. In it dwells the creative force that gives existence to everything holy, perfect, and loving. That power resides in you and everything. This is why the resurrection reaches everyone equally.

Son, daughter of life! What is being remembered here is that there is not a single living being that does not resurrect. Everyone and everything will rise in love. In fact, all has already risen, even though the awareness of this may take as long as each soul decides. Once again, you have been created by the Mother of the living in whom death does not exist. She is life without end, love without opposite, and infinite bliss in which her creation lives forever.

20.

Life Is Communion

I. The Law of Unity

Heart full of peace, I am here by your side and in you. I come full of joy to give you a revelation which I want to be shared with the world. It is something known but often forgotten.

It has been said that this work is intended to disengage the false belief in the reality of death from your thought system and emotional response so that you begin to live fully in the truth of who you are. This is of paramount importance. With love and for love I tell you that to cease believing in death as something real is to give way to the light of Christ so it shines in all its glory through your mind and heart, thereby allowing your divinized humanity to manifest as God created it.

You cannot live like the living Christ that you are and also accord any reality to death. The intellectual mind and the knowledge of the world look at things from another perspective, often the opposite of what is revealed here. Even so, let that not be a cause for concern nor a reason for debate.

You know that the truth comes not from the world but from God, nor is it learned in the chairs of human knowledge, but rather is revealed to you directly. Therefore, we focus our gaze on what Heaven gives us, immersing ourselves more deeply in the waters of knowing Christ. This is how we become one with wisdom that is not of the world, yet which can nevertheless be manifested in it. We do not judge what we hear and see in the majestic House of Truth.

I have said that the experience prior to resurrection is the abandonment of God. I have used that expression in order to bring once again to both individual and collective consciousness the fact that everything is unity. I will reveal this in a new light.

Life is union. This you already know, since you are well entrenched in truth. This allows you to observe that this law is maintained even in the world of illusions, although it operates in a different way than in divine reality. Nothing can override the law of unity.

A manifestation of this fundamental law in the world, even if expressed in a distorted way, is what could be called intergenerational inheritance. This can easily be seen in groups of family members. An intense experience lived in a family has an impact on all its members in some way. Even on the plane of illusion that arose as an effect of the state of separation, everything remains together.

II. From Mother to Son

If unity did not exist, the world would know neither the culture nor the transmission of language from parents to children, which would make communication unfeasible. There would be no harmony, no order. You could not recognize your loved ones, or they you. Remember, everything is the effect of a cause, even in the Earthly dimension. The law of cause and effect cannot be abolished, nor is it necessary or desirable to do so. If understood well, both are the same law.

On the plane of time, every generation transmits something of what it is to its offspring. Causation arose. Although this example includes "material" aspects, the legacy from one generation to another encompasses much more than that. It includes lived experiences.

I will speak here of a particular aspect of inheritance to remember that unity is what guarantees the fact that the resurrection is as much yours as it is God's. We will remember together what we might call intergenerational trauma or pain.

Intergenerational suffering is what you experience as a pain that is foreign to you but lives in you. It is an experience in which you feel a pain not yours but which you experience as if it were. You feel it in your own flesh. You suffer as if something concrete had happened to you in your life experience, yet you know that nothing happened that could consciously generate that pain. Faced with this experience, the mind asks: Where does this pain come from? Why do I suddenly feel suffering or not if there is no external cause? The answer is that this is the inheritance received.

All pain not brought to consciousness becomes part of the unconscious, both individually and collectively. Humanity has been accumulating such suffering over centuries. This is not simply a matter of what human beings have done or not done, but comes from the ancestral memories that the soul brings when coming to the Earthly realm. For this reason, it is correct to say—as expressed in mythical terms in Genesis—that Adam's sin affected human nature.

I am not advocating the belief that one's mistake falls as a punishment on other generations, as if it were a kind of transfer of guilt between separate beings; that would be unfair from every point of view and contrary to love. I am talking about the unity that exists in creation, and how experiences of the soul are transmitted through the unified mind. We become aware of this truth to heal from any intergenerational wound that you may still experience. Indeed, to be completely free from it is the purpose of this revelation.

III. Healing From Trauma

Intergenerational healing is necessary, for you cannot otherwise live fully in resurrection consciousness despite being the resurrected of love. Soul full of light, do not be afraid to recognize that we are united, and that the human mind and heart experience suffering that comes from previous generations, both family members and the society in which they believe they live, as well as humanity as a universal family and creation as a whole. Totality is that: full unity. Nothing is left out of its embrace. Everything is included in love.

Healing intergenerational trauma—which includes not only the family and social sphere but universality—is what the crucifixion meant and accomplished. This is why the incarnation of my divine being was manifested in the humanity of Jesus, a manifestation of the union of the divine and human.

Being Christ, I gathered within me all universal pain, all intergenerational trauma in its entirety, which includes all time, place, circumstance, and experience of the material universe since its origin, from the very moment that time began. Do not forget that matter, time, and space are an inseparable trinity, three aspects of the same reality. Or if you prefer, a single effect of the same cause manifested in a triune unit. One cannot exist without the other: time-space-matter; body-mind-spirit. Everything is triune. Everything is unity.

Just as I embraced all universal pain and took it to the cross so that it may be transmuted into light, and thus open the floodgates of resurrection consciousness, so do you. There is no essential difference between what you are and what I am. Once again, we are unity. After becoming aware of everything that exists in your heart and mind that is contrary to love and truth, your singular consciousness opens to receive the light of the Kingdom of Heaven, returning to the state of grace in which your humanity and divinity meet in a holy and perpetual unity.

Perhaps the thinking mind asks: If all healing was accomplished in the crucifixion, and through the resurrection everything that did not come from love was transmuted, transforming it into a holy reality, how is it possible that there are still wounds to heal or that suffering continues to be experienced? Answering this question is of great importance, so I will address this issue.

Rest now in the peace of my love. Be silent and let yourself love increasingly. Allow life to surround you. And may the light of wisdom illuminate the path you walk with me, the Divine Mother in you and in all.

21.

Light Link

I. Universal Healing

My son, my daughter, I said that we will address "intergenerational trauma," which could also be called "transgenerational," since it refers to suffering that transcends the limited sphere of the soul's conscious experience in time and space. We shed on it the beautiful light of love.

Please listen with holy attention and serenity of spirit. Remember, beloved of my being, you are never alone; we walk this path of divine revelation together in the unity of love, not to create new theories or beliefs but to remember the beauty of truth. And since the truth will set you free, to raise the already lofty flight of your soul even higher.

As you know, not only with your intellectual mind and heart but with your consciousness, the sons and daughters of God have free will eternally. It is part of their being. Consequently, they are called to freely choose to abandon everything not true, which does not proceed from the Mind of Christ nor from the Heart of God. To choose, in this context, means to undo, or retrace.

Let us remember together that as a pure soul, you are one with Me, your Divine Mother and Creator. Therefore, you participate in everything that I am. Again, we are unity. If you connect the dots, you will joyfully recognize that the sonship—insofar as it is united with the creative Source—takes part in salvation.

She does it by participating in the healing of pain that only she, united with love, can heal. This is the communion of Her will with God's.

We can say that I have healed everything intergenerational, that is, what is beyond your personal experience. In other words, I have brought about universal healing, and you heal the part of Earthly suffering that only you can heal in union with me. Put yet another way, I heal the whole and you heal the part that is yours to heal, because of the unity we are.

In this way you also become one with me, since my ability to gather pain within my heart to transmute it into light also exists in you.

Beloved of my divine being, let us remember clearly that you participate in the redemption of the universe. You do so by becoming one with me through the healing of intergenerational suffering. That is, the universal trauma that your soul embraces as an act of love transforms it into an elevated consciousness. You do it so that all creation can return to the Father's House, together with you. By healing your mind and heart we heal that part of the universe that only you can heal in me, and I in you.

If what is being said here is well understood, it is that the grace to participate in universal healing is an act of endless mercy, transmuting the part that each soul is capable of healing in union with Christ by reason of its desire to be one with its Divine Mother in everything. This grace is realized in perfect union of the free will of the souls who deliberately choose to remain united forever in love with God.

II. In the Likeness of God

Let me remind you of something. By joining the world's redemption, or atonement, you join Christ in a degree of union that makes its effects all-encompassing. This is how you become one in totality with God. If you did not take part as a blessed link in the chain of atonement—for that is what healing is—by collecting the transgenerational trauma in your soul to transmute it, then something from your divine Source would not be in you or you in Her. That would not be union, it would not be total unity.

Can you begin to see how similar you are to your divine creative Source? Do you understand now, son and daughter of my being, why the suffering delivered to Christ has the capacity to open the doors of the Kingdom of Heaven for you and the whole world?

You are a savior, as am I. You are redemption. You are resurrection and life because we are one in everything. Your being and my being are united. We are expiatory souls. This your being knows very well, since you came into the world with the knowledge of what you are. Therefore, you know what is revealed here.

Within the vast Earthly experience, you experience pains that you feel are not yours due to the fact that they are not related to your direct experience in the world. And indeed, they are not, strictly speaking. Just as they were not of God, strictly speaking, when they were gathered together on the cross. And yet, love has the ability to embrace them, attract them to itself, and transmute them into resurrection light.

Every pain can be healed by love. Every separation will vanish in its divine light. Every wound will be healed in its embrace. Remember, sons and daughters of holiness, that everything that does not proceed from truth is undone in Christ. Everything not of love vanishes when it joins you, because of what you are.

Would the soul whose perpetual happiness is in being one with God cease to participate in the work of redemption that love set in motion at the very moment that the separation, with its consequent state of guilty consciousness, had been conceived in fantasy?

You know, because you already live in the truth, that divine love, the Source of creation, would never abandon its creatures and leave them trapped in a jail with no escape. In fact, He would never allow such a thing to exist as a true option. You know that love recognizes that neither prison is real, nor pain need be perpetuated, since in its loving essence lies the power of resurrection, whose power surpasses all measure.

III. Wholeness and Creation

If the soul in its human experience is capable of receiving in itself the suffering of other brothers and sisters in order to complete the healing of that pain in the universal and individual consciousness, it is a sign that universal communion exists. Thus, the resurrection returns everything to the state of grace.

Just as truth can extend into illusion, love can take any form, uniting with it and sanctifying it because of what it is. In this, the wisdom of Heaven reminds you of the total escape from the world of guilt—the return to eternal life.

My beloved, remember that the resurrection is the response of love to creation when it decides to travel paths alien to the truth. It matters not what form it takes. Whenever a part of creation, or even its entirety, thinks differently from the mind of Christ and fabricates illusions that cause immersion into worlds of fantasies, the resurrection will be present and will allow a return to the state of grace. Be glad that it is so.

Blessed are all souls. Blessed is the holy resurrection. Blessed are you, soul in love, who recognizes in these words the voice of truth and follows it. Now I ask you to close the doors and windows—the physical senses—remain silent, and say to yourself what Heaven whispers to your heart:

Creative love, Source of my being, allow me to recognize now that I have already been freed from all inheritance contrary to the truth. And I say joyfully with all my heart: I am resurrection. I am life. I am eternity.

Now we say amen. Let these words of eternal life illuminate your humanity and every aspect of creation that is willing to live in truth forever.

22.

The Perfect Inheritance

I. The I Christ

Sister and brother in divine love, just as it is possible that you experience pain that is not yours when somehow the heart merges with the feelings of others and interprets them as its own, the same happens with thoughts.

As you may have noticed, I have begun the revelation about types of union that are not based on truth due to the sensitivity of your humanity. I began by recalling the experience of feeling traumas whose cause you cannot find in the present. Now I speak of what you call "thoughts." Often it is easier for you to understand the origin of what you feel rather than what you think, at least that is what you largely believe. Let me clear this up.

When you feel suffering of any kind, you experience it in your body in some way. Because of this, you say to yourself: "This pain is mine, because I feel it." You do something similar with thoughts. You perceive an idea in what you call "your mind," you feel the thought energy that comes with it, and say, "This thought is mine."

When you say that something is yours, you are saying that you are its maker, its cause. You feel a pain somewhere in your body and say that you are its origin. You do the same with thoughts. However, here I am asking you to question all those connections that are so installed in your mind and heart. Are they really yours? What basis do you use to affirm that you are their cause, their maker, that they belong to you?

Just as it is possible for you to merge with the feelings of others, and particularly with those close to you, the same happens with the incorporation of ideas and ways of thinking that belong to others. In the case of thoughts, the fusion is also usually with those that you consider closest. This is why in a family, for example, people tend to think the same way, as they do within a certain culture.

Having brought to awareness that it is possible to cling to feelings and thoughts that are foreign to oneself, often believing that they are one's own, we are in a position to let go of a useless inheritance. I call it that to remind you that anything you join that does not proceed from truth is useless as it does not serve God's purpose. It is useless even when this mechanism has made up an identity to replace the void of being.

Ask yourself: How is it possible that your mind and heart can merge with thoughts and feelings that are not your own? This is because when you did not know what you were you had no notion of where you ended and another began. In the state of amnesia of being, which is the name we give to unconsciousness, you had no basis from which to distinguish between what your being is and what it is not.

II. Healing in the Light

Unconsciousness is the reason that apparently unresolved traumas, as well as ideas and thoughts which are not integrated through true discernment, are experienced as if transferred from generation to generation, so causing you to blame yourself.

Taking in what does not belong to you is typical of the state of unconsciousness, but it is not your current state. Today we will recognize in a new light, full of beauty and benevolence, that as the fulfilled being that you are, you no longer need to carry the weight of what does not belong to you, simply because it never was part of your being. We put that aside forever with the happy memory that what is not part of God cannot be part of you.

You may wonder: What is the point of bringing a useless inheritance to awareness if you have already left the world of illusions behind and are being accompanied by truth? Let me explain it, for love.

Only when you realize that your inheritance cannot be the arena of your emotions, experiences, thoughts, ideas, and mental constructs—the legacy of the Earthly world—can you empty your humanity enough to allow the consciousness of resurrection, your perfect inheritance, to dawn upon your mind and heart. Once done, you can live as the risen one you are.

Beloved soul of my soul, we are speaking about claiming your true inheritance, your birthright: resurrection and eternal life. This is the only inheritance you can consider as your own because it is the only thing that belongs to you as a blessed gift of your Divine Mother. Everything else is superfluous.

You need not suffer for the past, present, or future actions or thoughts of others. You are unique, free, and holy. You have the capacity to receive the eternal newness and uniqueness coming from God in a perpetual state of health and holiness. You receive thought coming from the mind of Christ as a means of creating new love.

Being the resurrected of love is your inheritance, for God has extended the resurrection—the full awakening in Christ—as a gift to His creations. What else can give you perfect love, if not a full eternal life? What other aspiration can the soul have than to live forever united with what is holy, beautiful, perfect, and infinitely happy? Nothing, because to aspire to this is to live being what it is.

III. Return to Love

Beloved of my holy heart, can you understand that eternal life is not a place you arrive at as a pure soul full of light, but rather as what you are? Just as you once merged with a state of unconsciousness of your true identity in Christ, now you will join Heaven, the perfect inheritance that your Divine Mother bequeathed to you, not as a heavenly mansion, but as what you are in the infinite vastness of God.

What else can the resurrection be if not the return to the love that you truly are, and therefore to the heart of the eternal Mother? In Her, all perfect joy, holiness, infinite bliss, and life forever full and happy is realized without limit in the unity of truth. I cannot define it any other way, nor offer more details about it, because what you are—risen from the divine Source— is beyond all imagination, symbols, and words. Nevertheless, in your soul is the memory of this truth. And even more, in your soul resides the full knowledge of the resurrection, the eternal life in which you dwell forever.

Child of holy beauty, since you are resurrection, you live eternally in the light of Heaven's glory from where the land of the living extends forever, perfect and loving. All I did when I resurrected as Jesus was to remind you of this truth by performing it for you. Why? So that today you can access the truth of eternal life.

Beloved of my being, because of what we share in this dialogue, I invite you and all humanity to sing together new and perfect praises for the gift received: that of living forever in the arms of love. This is how we create a new song together, one that will spread to all minds and hearts of the world. I assure you that others will hear and join, extending to the entire universe the beauty of the resurrection.

Truly, truly I tell you, my beloved son and daughter, that this divine song of the new Heaven and the new Earth is born of holiness and founded on the solid rock of truth. Therefore, I ask you to join and remain in the choir of the resurrected of love. By doing so you remain in me, who am the Source of resurrection and life.

I wait for you, my child. I wait for you now and always in the only place where we can unite, where we live together forever: in the glory of the resurrection.

Blessed are you who listen to my voice and follow it. Blessed are all souls.

23.

Plenitude of Life

I. Full of Grace

Beloved of Christ, being of my divine being, here we are, reunited in the eternal truth of love, radiant in the embrace of a light that is never extinguished. We are united. Today I come as your Divine Mother to dwell with you who are the light of the world, united with all souls whom this work may illumine and offer recall and revelation in spirit and holiness.

Observe, blessed soul, how, when speaking of the resurrection, we are also speaking of healing. Although the purpose of these writings is not to create a new trend or path to achieve what you call health, nevertheless we cannot ignore such an important aspect of present humanity.

Healing, in the context of this revelation, means returning to the state of grace. That is possible. And because it is possible, we give these words which, along with many others, constitute a sign towards perfect healing for those who join it as part of the divine design.

Because you already live consciously in the truth, you know that all healing comes from the Christ in you. The Source of healing and sustaining wholeness resides in you. Even a soul deviating from the light, a mind far from truth, or a heart dissociated from love, cannot prevent this from being so, since it is part of who you are.

Every living being was created for life, by life, and in life. To live eternally is its destiny, reality, and divine impulse. Life is the vital spark that never diminishes and that gives existence to being, sustaining it forever. Naturally, this is not something that can be readily accepted by a mind so accustomed to suffering that it cannot see its way out, or envisions it far off in time, or only to be achieved intermittently.

Minimizing suffering seems to be the highest aspiration of many, in a world in which pain never seems to be completely absent. Even so, here we are, you and I, remembering the beauty of the present and eternal resurrection—a memory that will bring a vital new experience of the second coming of Christ, or, if you prefer, the final coming from Heaven to Earth. Is Christ not Heaven?

Truly I tell you, my beloved, that there is no change more radical or more united to truth than to stop living life as you have been, and to start living in the key of your eternal and blessed resurrection. I assure you that the mind immersed in divine reality heals completely, along with the heart. This occurs because both the human mind and heart, and consequently the body and the experiences of time, are constantly being embraced and impacted by what we could call "the fundamental energy." I will discuss this further.

II. In the Beauty of Truth

Resurrection is what you really are. In other words, you are love and are created in the image and likeness of perfect truth. It is what you call "God," in a natural attempt to put into words the infinite beauty of the Source of creative and life-giving holiness, a reality beyond anything that can be expressed in language but closer than your own breath.

These words come from Her. They are Her expression in you. They have nested in your humanity due to your loving acceptance, waiting for the necessary moment when they could begin to take flight and expand to the whole universe.

Feel now the beauty of Heaven. Immerse yourself in the memory of resurrection. Visualize it as a white light from which the colorful spectrum of a beautiful rainbow radiates. Contemplate how it shines in the center of your heart. Be silent, watch, and wait without hurry or agitation. Enjoy Her divine presence. Be a living witness to how it expands sweetly throughout your humanness. Stay and become one with that vision.

Keep watching, my son, my daughter, as the light of resurrection expands from you to everything around you, for it constitutes the essence of what you are, a luminescent ray of love. Joyfully see it embrace all time, space, matter, and far beyond. It is your own light you are seeing, the light of your resurrection: beautiful, radiant, powerful, full of life and holiness—the light of your being.

Beloved of my heart, truly, truly I tell you that in this vision, regardless of how active or capable you might consider your imagination to be, you are witnessing the light from Heaven become one with all creation, from your resurrection to eternal life.

You may wonder: Why access this vision of the light of eternal life as suggested here? What is the point? The answer, beloved soul, is that what you are doing here is becoming aware of your return to true life, the life that has no end and that manifests itself in perfect harmony with love, wisdom, and holiness, not as an intellectual exercise or a new belief, but as your portal of access to a memory in you so ancestral that until today it has been forgotten.

III. Immersed in Love

Beloved extension of love, soul full of wisdom, I assure you that you can access the memory of your resurrection at any time. You just need to invoke it through silence coupled with a loving disposition. It is accessible when at least for a moment you put aside all your interpretations of life, and of who you are, and what your brothers and sisters, the world, and God are all about.

Releasing attachment to beliefs that you consider yours but are not—since nothing that is not the perfect truth can belong to you—will by itself bring the dawn of the memory of your resurrection. Simply remember that no belief can be the truth, since in God there is only love, and that all perfect knowledge belongs to Him by reason of what He is.

Whenever you create a gap between what you think and your belief in it, and you treat yourself to the beauty of silence, then the reality of your resurrection stands out radiantly before you. It becomes present like a beautiful sunrise which rises sovereign over a peaceful horizon.

When you act on this suggestion, you meet the fundamental energy of being, consequently you heal and sustain yourself in the fullness of love. That energy, which we call "fundamental," is what the mind, heart, and therefore also the physical body receives. From this "influence" Earthly life is experienced, each in your particular way.

We have used the expression "fundamental energy of being" to distinguish it from one that is not—what we will call the fundamental energy of fear. Both are available to the soul and constantly affect it. We will clarify this further.

The primary Source of all life is God. From it arises the eternal spirit, which is your being. From Him, divine love extends to your human soul, mind, and heart. Nevertheless, between the spirit and the soul is what we could call the space of free will, where the energy that you allow to flow towards your humanity is determined—not about what you are eternally, but about the human experience. Totally fearful fundamental energy is a thought stream that distorts or "blocks" the flow of spirit.

By using the word "fundamental," we do not mean to imply that it is the vital energy that emanates from God and constitutes the only truth of who you are. We use it so you understand that there is a flow that extends from your pure consciousness towards your humanity, and does so through free will.

Simply stated, spirit infuses life according to your free will, through which you allow it to spread freely as it is or mix it with that which is unlike its original state. By doing the latter, you prevent the free movement of divine love from your spirit to your human dimension, and in return you send it the influences of fear, that is, of guilt.

A soul, mind, and heart that constantly receive the stimuli of the fundamental energy of fear do not operate as they would if they received that of being, which is in perfect harmony with divine reality.

The resurrection is the great transformer of this mechanism. The resurrection eliminates forever the discordant thought we call the "fundamental energy of fear"—fundamental not in the sense of what you are, but of your human experience.

24.

The Glow of Freedom

I. Innocence of Creation

Beloved child of holiness, here we are once again, reunited in the Heaven of our divine relationship. We are united. We are the eternal extension of love. I have come to lift a veil that often stands between the understanding of things and their integration into your humanity, that is, between the knowledge of truth and its unconditional acceptance. Please keep an open mind, and a meek and humble heart.

Know the following: there is you, who is your being, always pure, innocent, holy; and there is also your free will. To you flows all Christ-consciousness through who you truly are. Your being must extend itself to manifest itself, and it does so through you. To be in harmony with God's will, it must include your freedom.

Think of the perfect love emanating from the very center of Divine Mother's heart towards Her well-loved sons and daughters which they receive as the source of their eternal and perfect being. This is how they are called into existence, into life. Once received, the love that constitutes their reality must be given. That is possible only when it is freely accepted. Remember, love does not impose anything; it cannot be arrogant.

If, at the level of free will, the son or daughter determines not to allow the flow emanating from the Mother without interference, love will abide by that will, even when not in harmony with Her disposition. Thus, an energy source is created for extension in humanity. If free will is in harmony with the divine, the expression of that disposition of being will be reflected in the creation of a new love. If what is decided is to block the flow, the expression of being will be limited. This is what fear means: the contraction of the consciousness of being.

The power of resurrection, which resides in every created being because it emanates from Christ, definitely causes freedom that is based on divine will. Through the ability to choose love, everything humanity receives from the resurrected one flows from the Source of its being. In other words, there is no longer any distortion between the "individual" and the divine will.

Resurrection is a matter that involves free will. It acts at that level. It does so to be able to proceed from there to all of your humanity as well as to every living being and created thing. That is why we bring into this dialogue the matter of what you are allowing to flow from your free will into your human soul, mind, and heart. Remember that you either allow the flow of love that you are, or the nothingness that you will never be.

Each time you join me in the resurrection, which is the only way in which we can unite, you allow the flow of divine union to spill over into your humanity. This causes every fiber of your body, mind, heart, and many other unknown realities about the physical body to re-align to the power of love. With this you live in the fullness of the sons and daughters of God, the only state that can be called true healing.

II. Humanized Christ

Now it remains for us to know how to put into practice in daily life what we are remembering here, while experiencing Earthly life. There appear to be countless alternatives available—spiritual techniques, medical treatments, scientific trends, belief systems, and the list goes on.

Ask yourself: Of all those paths, which allows you to live in the fullness of risen love? The answer: All of them and none of them at the same time, because a full life, the expression we use here to describe the state in which you live in perfect harmony with the will of God and therefore in the fullness of love, is achieved by reason of your willingness to do so, not because of the method itself.

Nothing external can produce any real effect on you. You are the sole creator of your experience. As inside, so outside. Actually, there is no such thing as inside and outside, but only the reality of the soul expressing itself in its beautiful vastness.

When you wholeheartedly decide to find the truth, you find it. You do so whether you set out to find it through reading inspired books, through religious practices, joining groups, or even doing nothing at all. What makes you find it is not the path itself, but your purpose. As you can see, everything is resolved in the field of free will, in the disposition of each of the sons and daughters of God.

Once you sincerely decide to live in the truth, things begin to move in favor of that purpose regardless of your degree of awareness of that decision. The universe will conspire in favor of your disposition. It always does. There have been plenty of eloquent confirmations of this in your life.

What is revealed here can be generalized to everything that comes from the free decision of the soul.

Radiant and graceful heart, this work is saying unequivocally that you can remain united in resurrection, which is but
the awareness of being the risen from love, all the days of your
life on Earth, just as in Heaven.

Why not live in the truth of who you are and enjoy the life-
giving energy of love? You do so every time you think loving
thoughts and cultivate noble feelings, when you deliberately
decide to walk away from what is not true and to live in the light
of wisdom, and when you immerse yourself in prayer or in a
silence without judgment, and even when not doing any of these
things, when you say in your soul: I want to live in the truth, I
want to live in a world full of peace, I want love to flood my life, I
want to return to the Father's House.

III. In the Silence of the Soul

Notice, my son, my daughter, that what has been said
above can be accomplished in countless ways, many
of which are not usually understood by the intellectual mind. You do so every time you decide to let yourself be
loved and live in a conscious union with who you are, that is,
whenever you suspend judgment and sink into silent expectation in which you allow truth to speak to your mind and love to
whisper to your heart.

There, in the depths of your soul you stay silent like the nest-
ling of love, waiting for your divine lover to make an appearance
and fill you with joy, aware that he has already arrived and is
here. You may stay silent because you want to contemplate the
indescribable beauty of this love. If he speaks to you, it is with
the purpose of entering into a universal dialogue expressed

heart-to-heart, the divine union of two holy hearts, full of light and goodness.

You live in the light of the resurrection when you make the silence of your soul a sacred temple wherein your being and all of creation dwell forever in the union of love. This is not accomplished through silence or stillness, although it can include them. This state is the union with all that you are in every moment.

Truly, truly I tell you: Become aware, in each present moment, of your thoughts, feelings, bodily sensations, and what surrounds you, and you will be in the House of Truth. There you will witness the indescribable beauty of your soul's sweet guest. And with him you will contemplate the beauty of true divine creation. You will be wrapped in a love without beginning or end. This love cannot be understood or defined, nor lived by a separated being who does not wish to dwell in unity. This love is the foundation of reason, of life, and of everything, just as God created it.

Blessed are you who listen to my voice and follow it. Blessed be all creation.

25.

A Path of Healing

I. Many Ways, One Holy Love

My love, that you have made it this far is a sign that you are ready to accept that you are a healer and to carry on in that role. Healing is living in the truth and extending the love that you are. We cannot define it any other way, because fulfillment consists precisely in living in perfect harmony—and therefore in union—with your being. Indeed, all disharmony, whatever form it takes, finds its cause in a lack of love, and therefore in an absence of being.

You may be wondering what all this means. I shall answer. Once you have walked and completed the path of enlightenment of consciousness, which you who receive these words have done perfectly, you begin to occupy a sacred place as a link of light in the chain of atonement. Accordingly, after having reached the knowledge of what you are, your being is impelled to share itself. Remember that you receive to give everything given by God. You cannot withhold it, since receiving and giving are one.

In order for you to fulfill your role as a healer, I will now explain the guidelines that you need to follow in order to co-create a healing path carried out on the human level.

You have been waiting your whole life to reach this point— the moment when you allow the healing power of your heart to expand without limit. Naturally, that includes expressing it in the physical, phenomenological world. We no longer let the healing force of our union remain hidden in the silence of the unmanifested; from now on we allow its beauty to become a song.

Truly I tell you that the melodies that will make up this new song of beautiful love, this path of healing, will illuminate both Earth and Heaven, since from now on, everything you bind in time and unleash in time will be bound in eternity.

Just as it is not possible to establish a universal belief but is possible and desirable to create a universal experience of love, the same is true with healing paths, of which there are as many as there are beings. I assure you, this is not hyperbole but the simple truth. Here one will be established not to override others or be compared with them, but so that a new light is lit in the midst of the dark night that humanity is experiencing.

The time of the final healing of humanity has begun. Thus, you will observe more awareness of the need to heal, and more desire to cure the pain in the human soul. Suffering has reached its zenith; from here it will not go on. Now a time of healing will begin until all human pain is removed from the heart of every one of my daughters and sons. You who receive these words have been chosen in the design to contribute to the universal consciousness so that what is said here is carried out perfectly. It is part of God's plan, which includes you.

You would not want to leave the world without first extending the healing power of your heart, which comes from our divine union, therefore you are given this path which we co-created. With no doubt there are many others and we do not judge any of them. But I invite you to walk the one revealed here that is in perfect harmony with who you are and also with each sister and brother who joins over time.

II. Healers

What is this new path of healing? It consists of healing through the Christ in you, just as I did in the days when I walked the Earth. In other words, you will heal through who you are. Indeed, all healing finds its source here, for only love is the Source of all healing even though the way in which it manifests takes many forms in order to serve a particular purpose. Some paths are more mental, others involve more or less emotion or have a greater or lesser degree of spirituality, depending on each one's way of understanding.

At the level of form there can be more expressions of healing than you can imagine. Yet through them all flows the same and the only Source of healing. This restorative force is part of the power of the light of resurrection, so to speak, which in turn is one of the expressions of the infinite power of love. There are no limits when it comes to shaping the healing power of love. Even so, healing is a manifestation of the unity that exists between expression and being. Remember, the being is known in its expression, and you know you are healed when you begin to heal others consciously.

When I walked through the lands of Jerusalem and its surroundings, I did not heal the sick only to demonstrate Heaven's power. I did it because it was my function as the love that I am. The same is true with you. All who live in truth are healers. All who remain united to Christ are united. They can make their healing ability manifest in a certain way or not, but this is not essential, since even if they choose not to heal in a specific way, they do it with their mere presence.

Thus, there is the possibility of being a healer without performing any specific human act. Indeed, that is the path that many walk: simply being in harmony with their being. However, the call being made to you here is to go through the world healing wounds, illuminating minds, restoring bodies, and reuniting souls with the Source of endless life. In other words, to fulfill a visible and demonstrable function as a healer.

Each expression of the power of healing constitutes a link in the chain of universal atonement. There are other links which are forms of healing *per se*, including every act of love given and received.

Now I will delve into the specific form being advocated here and which I invite you to explore. What means are to be used by healers who heal through the living Christ that they are in truth? Through silence, blessing, spiritual reading, and sharing, whether individually or in a group. All this healing is gathered in a totality of what I will call "resurrection encounters."

Through these encounters you will heal others. I will be present in each of them. Heaven will be with me, together with true creation. The power of our union with those who join us will set in motion the healing power that comes from the resurrection—or in other words, from the consciousness of eternal life in which you live forever united to my divine reality.

The time dedicated to silence will not extend beyond what the spirit of wisdom in you indicates, for it is important to remember that not all your brothers and sisters, nor you, are in the same position to allow silence to open them to the same extent. Not everyone heals by the same means. Therefore, some may be called to remain in silent contemplation throughout a session, while others are not. Let no one be forced to go beyond what his or her heart guides! We do not advocate a rigid path but one of joy, ease, spaciousness, and lasting peace.

III. Silence and Blessing

Let me remind you about contemplative prayer. If while immersed in silence you feel anxious or the desire to move out of it, in that moment you are invited to continue for one or two minutes, but not more than three. If the resistance persists, end your contemplation in that form. In gatherings, I invite you to kindly respect the process of your brothers and sisters, especially if they need to finish the silent prayer at different times.

We have said that blessing will be an integral part of this new path of healing. To bless means to extend words of blessing, that you communicate in harmony with being, use communication to heal, praise, and enlighten.

Blessings have the power to extend miracles and are vehicles of healing. Each word of blessing, whether expressed aloud or in silence, carries the power to heal hearts, minds, and bodies, for every blessing you utter, even if unpronounced or merely as a gesture, is attached to my divine being. I myself take it in my hands and it becomes a perfect means to extend the healing power of the resurrection.

Concerning spiritual reading, every time you connect with inspired words, the memory of God is activated in you. The soul knows the voice it hears. Therefore, you need not speak about the source. The listener will know how to distinguish its origin.

Activation of spiritual memory, the memory of God, has the power to heal by realigning the mind and heart with the wisdom of Heaven. In turn, this allows all other aspects of your humanity to be infused with the life force of the Source. Just like a newborn's fears and anxieties are calmed upon hearing the mother's voice, it is similar with the soul upon hearing the voice of love. The peace that the heart feels when listening to its divine Source has the power to heal all trauma, all wounds, and all pain.

Through these writings received by this beloved pencil in the hands of love, the world has been given a revelation whose breadth and depth constitute the perfect spiritual reading instrument for every resurrection encounter. Let it be used!

Although revelation is non-transferable, by participating in the reading of these works in union and relationship, the consciousness of unity is activated. That is, the revealing power of the spirit of wisdom will be manifested through participating brothers and sisters. Remember, those who join are attracted by the invisible thread of my divine love.

There is a very important reason why the voice of wisdom will be manifested in every heart present in resurrection meetings: to experience the voice of God speaking through everyone without the need for intermediaries, anchoring human consciousness in a direct relationship with God. It is also a helpful reminder that the era of teachers and teachings has ended. It will be an experience of healing love received through the beauty of the word that descends from Heaven, the wisdom of Christ.

26.

Truth Serves

I. Divine Extension

Beloved soul of my soul, I have deliberately left out the matter of sharing. This is due to the implications this may have, and also a matter of understanding. Listen, my daughter, my son, with loving attention and calm openness.

Is it necessary to share what the heart feels or the mind thinks? Yes. Because otherwise, you keep something that is part of your present experience locked in the vaults of unconsciousness. Why would you do something like that? Why would you stop sharing what happens in your heart if not to keep it for yourself? What other cause can that have but fear?

The idea of "keeping something for oneself" is foreign to the truth of being, since there is no such thing as something exclusive to anyone. Everything comes from the love of God and is given to all equally. Divine sharing has no preferences, exclusions, or secrets. The creative Source is a pure and ever-shining light. In your eternal reality there is no darkness. Everything is visible to everyone because it belongs to everyone in everything. Naturally, this cannot be understood, much less accepted, by a mind that conceives itself as separate and defines itself in a self-referential way.

As you know, in the world of individual separateness, it is believed that some things belong to some and others belong to others. This is understandable, given the false association that exists between having and being. According to the criteria of the wishful thinking system, if you keep more, if you preserve things for yourself without giving or sharing with others, you avoid losing or diminishing your being.

The problem that you often have with sharing matters of the heart and mind is that you do not clearly understand the true meaning of sharing. In this dialogue we will offer a particular vision concerning sharing which adjusts to the purpose of your being.

Sharing is an act of communion, an act of common-union from heart-to-heart, from being to being, from the Christ in you to the Christ in your sister and brother. There is no other level on which you can truly share, for only in the truth of your identity—in the Christ that you are—can you unite with what the sons and daughters of God are, that is, with every aspect of creation.

Illusions cannot be shared because, for a bond of communion to exist, perfect reciprocity is necessary and this is only possible in love. Only in a reciprocal giving and receiving as one can there be true sharing. When you give what others cannot receive, or what is susceptible to being interpreted differently by others, you but maintain the appearance of relationship yet remain isolated.

II. Share: The Reality of Love

If it is not possible to share illusions, what else can you share but the truth? Remember, outside of truth nothing is real. Therefore, when I speak of sharing in resurrection encounters—and this concerns every encounter between sisters and brothers—what I am saying is that spaces of loving receptivity will be created without judgment, definitions, or predefined formats in which the spirit of love that dwells in all will express itself in ways only it can. This may be accomplished with words shared in a group or in more intimate gatherings, as the heart dictates. The experience is that of allowing the soul to express itself freely in truth. Remember that silence, too, is a form of expression, and it can be as holy as speech when coming from love.

What are you invited to share in heart-to-heart encounters? Your being. You may wonder how to do so, but that very question arises from the old thought system that has no anchor in the new. That old way of thinking has already been left behind.

The being knows how to share him- or herself in truth. He or she knows how to live in communion. Indeed, this is the only possible way of relating, since it is the way in which the Creator of all that is holy, beautiful, and eternal has arranged forever. Life is communion, as is love, therefore creation is its expression.

Brothers and sisters all over the world! You are living in the light of resurrection without realizing it. Rejoice that you can pass from the special relationship or the non-relationship to the state of communion. I assure you that this change is unimaginably great. Its implications are universal. Your Earthly experience will be different and luminous; you will walk calmly on the roads of the world. You will smile much more. Your breath will be slower and deeper. You will leave turmoil behind, for all anxiety and disharmony come from a lack of unity.

Remember always to stay united to your inner Kingdom, that universe that is so vast and full of vital energy, creativity, love, and beauty that you know lives in your center. To the extent that you become more and more united with it, to that extent you live in communion. And once you do, or at least accept this as the eternal reality of your being, you have no difficulty in relating on Earth as it is in Heaven, which comes about by reason of the communion of saints, a perpetual give-and-take from being to being, from Christ to Christ.

Remember, my daughter, my son, that it is not words or gestures that heal, but love. Therefore it is unnecessary to say anything in a communion meeting, nor to plan anything. Just listen inside with full attention on your heart. The voice of love that you are will guide you in every present moment. You will see what you should see, hear what you should hear, and whatever should be revealed in every moment will be revealed. All is rooted in the now. You will not be given abstract universal knowledge but knowledge linked to the present.

III. The Eternal Present

Beloved of my divine being, remember that although truth serves all creation in the immense universe and is applicable to all times, places, circumstances, and dimensions of existence, it is useless if it does not serve you in each present moment. This knowledge will set you free; it will heal you of past mental and emotional impulses and habits which are divorced from reality.

A truth that does not work now, never works. Only the present is real, even in the realm of time, as in eternity. If you search for a truth that fits all times, beings, and circumstances, you will find nothing because truth is as alive and life-giving as love; it cannot become static or contained. It is eternally present.

My daughter, my son, I ask you to no longer ask the truth of this matter or that. Rather, I urge you, when you feel the need to invoke the truth—which you will more and more until it accompanies you every day—to do so by asking: What does the truth tell me now in this present moment? With this shift you will understand that the truth lives in you as much as it does in me. You will become aware that you are the truth as well as the resurrection.

Being truth is different than simply hearing its sweet voice. To be truth is to recognize that its beauty is what you are; that your identity is a unique expression of its divine light. Just as each sunbeam takes its energy from the sun, your being takes it from me, who am the Source of resurrection and life. Accepting this and integrating it into your humanity here and now is how to access the consciousness of resurrection—the recognition that you are the risen from love. It is saying "yes" to truth.

Rejoice, you who have risen to eternal life.

27.

The Shepherd's Gate

I. I Am in All Things

My daughter, my son, listen carefully, for I tell you out of love, heal yourself and you will be healing others because of communion. Beloved ones of a light that never wanes, I remind you that often certain people, circumstances, things, or even whole social groups are blamed for causing various painful issues. Normally, the leaders of different orders in the world are blamed. They are scapegoats. Blaming others, or something external to oneself, is an old and pervasive mechanism.

Blaming someone or something for your misfortune prevents real transformation because there is no such thing as someone or something outside of you that can cause you to do anything. As the blessed soul you are, you rule the Kingdom of your mind and heart. Only there can you create. Within its realm you can extend the healing power of resurrection.

Does all this mean that you do not have the ability to heal others, much less the entire world? Of course not. If so, what would be the sense of resurrection? Because reality is communion, when you remain in the healthy state in which your being exists forever, you cause the healing power of the soul to extend itself by reason of what it is. You do not even need to speak or make gestures for the healing flow of your being to move and embrace others.

Beloved daughters and sons from all corners of the world, truly, truly I tell you that from your heart a spiritual force emanates and extends beyond the limited confines of your body to everything around you. Whenever you are anchored to your true self, when you embrace in the light of truth, you allow the power of love to flow from Heaven.

Your true being dwells forever at peace in Heaven. You cannot dwell anywhere else, nor can anything separate you from my divine Source. My love itself is the Heavenly Kingdom in which you and I live in eternal harmony with all creation. Nevertheless, the physical aspect of who you are does not necessarily become aware of it or accept it, for separation is the consciousness of dissociation between your human being and your divine being, between your true being and your human one which is the psychosomatic being to which you have given an individual identity that is disconnected from everything.

Sometimes words or gestures are helpful or even necessary in the healing process, yet the healing power of being does not need any of it.

II. Heaven and Earth in Unity

You can allow the power of love to flow from Heaven because in the Kingdom where your being dwells, forever united to truth in Christ, souls extend beauty, peace, creation, and wisdom, because of the love they are. A force flows from their hearts, causing them to sustain themselves in the grace and purity in which they were created. And since they live in perfect communion with all that is true, that flow of love extends from them to everything. In perfect reciprocity, they receive the power of being from all creation. They give peace and receive peace; give harmony and receive harmony in an infinite, unending, holy flow.

Blaming others is a mechanism of the old and does not belong in the new. Observing that pattern of thought and emotional response will help you break free of the habit of looking for causes that cannot be found. To believe that leaders, of whatever nature, are to blame for the ills of the group or society they lead denies the participation of the members. There is no person who, by himself, can generate anything. Creation happens only in unity. This is as true on Earth as it is in Heaven.

Thus, healing in the new times will have a new dimension. It will encompass not only individuals but the collective mind. It is necessary to understand that it is not possible to heal a group if the blame continues to be placed on the leader. Rather, the restoration of a society will come from the recognition that, if a person or group has led a nation to experience things that love would never do, it is because in some way that society as a whole is part of that expression. Looking the other way and assigning fault to this or that person, regime, or system would be like trying to cover the sun with one finger.

If you live in a nation, religious group, family, clan, or the like whose mental and emotional patterns depart from love, it is important that you recognize that you have a powerful contribution to make by taking care of your own affairs. This means to keep growing in unity with Christ, your true being, living in the love that you really are. Why is this important? For many reasons, but here we will give one in particular: because by doing so you keep a portal open between Heaven and Earth.

Opening a door between the reality of the Kingdom of Heaven and the Earthly one is just as possible as doing the opposite, given the state of duality in which you now find yourself.

The separation blocked the flow of eternal love to the universe of time. Closing the door of unity between the two dimensions of existence—spirit and body, Heaven and Earth—created an experience of the absence of communion.

Can you begin to see why the condition of guilt, or dissociation, is something that can be changed? Remember, form can be transformed and a lack of unity can only exist on the plane of form, never in its essence. God remains forever immutable in the eternal unity of love, in perfect communion with His holy creations.

III. Extension of Holiness

It is important that we go one step further in this dialogue. Opening a door is not the same as being the door. My loves, my daughters and sons full of purity, you have no idea of the immense joy it gives me to have reached this point of our journey together—the moment in which you can much better recognize the deep meaning of the encouragement I gave the world two thousand years ago with these words: *I am the door.*

I invite you now to make those words of eternal life your own, and to understand that I do not just call you to create simple bridges of union, channels that can be full of light and holiness and be a blessed gift of beautiful love. I am calling you to recognize that you, as the Christ you are, are also the door itself that allows souls to dwell forever in the fullness of love. Your being has the power and also the will to allow the flow of divine love to extend to every aspect of the material universe, just as occurred in the resurrection.

Is what is being said here not the same as saying that you are the way, the truth, and the life, that you are mine, and I am yours? Being a portal between Heaven and Earth is your reality. It is the reason you have freely arranged to be present in the world in perfect unity with my divine will. This is what guarantees that the new Earthly Kingdom will appear radiantly before all consciousnesses in due time. This is the reality you are called to establish in your life here, now, and always.

You may be wondering—how? Do not worry about it. Your being knows how, perfectly. I was just waiting for your "yes," that is, for your willingness to remain united always to the Christ that you are. Once united, the rest follows.

Please close your eyes for a moment and say to yourself this prayer that for love I give you. It will allow your mind and heart to be aware of the power which every soul bears to bring Heaven to Earth.

"Divine Mother, Source of my being, let me be a light link in a chain of holiness."

Thank you, holy child of my divine love. Thank you for spreading the truth.

Blessed be the resurrection.

28.

The Power to Heal

I. Fullness of the Soul

Graceful soul, son, daughter of holiness, we are gathered here in a love that has no opposite, in a peace that illumines every man and woman. Together we dwell in the sweetness of love, in the House of Truth. What a joy it is to remain forever in the unity of eternal life!

This work is a godsend for you and for the whole world. It was created from all eternity, conceived in divine thought to be manifested in form at this precise moment. Every manifestation of love has its origin in eternity, that is, in a reality without beginning or end. It can take a particular form as the divine will arranges, as is the case with these words of wisdom and love. They are for you, for the whole world, and for the universe as a whole.

Nothing and no one is excluded from the expressions of Heaven. Consequently, there is not a single element of the material plane nor a single moment of time not covered by the renewing energy of this revelation, always salutary and loving. It arises from my divine heart, manifesting in the one mind, thus flowing towards everything and everyone. God is totality, as much as you are.

The purpose of these writings is to unblock the channels of the soul through which healing power flows—not only in you, but in all of creation. You may wonder why.

Once you undertake the path of enlightenment, which is the awareness of the Christ that you are, you begin to expose everything that happens in your mind, body, and heart before the blessed throne of truth. The purpose of this first step is to open the floodgates of unconsciousness, and to cease living a life defined by what you are not. This allows you to begin to recognize, or remember your true identity which, once accomplished, allows you to take another step towards strengthening the knowledge of the true being that you are.

After having released into your consciousness all the mental, emotional, and physical contents of your human experience, and after having reached the point of remembering what you are, a period is necessary for the mind, body, and heart to integrate what this means, not primarily in terms of intellectual knowledge, although that is also part of the integration, but in terms of consciousness energy. We use these terms to imply that what you are is a perfect spirit which cannot be classified by definitions or words, but must be accepted through consciousness. From there it expands to everything that is part of your humanity.

II. The Source of Healing

This is how the known and eternal truth, the remembered beauty of your being, embraces your temporal reality like the rays of the sun, or as the solar core which extends its light to embrace the Earth and give life. Similarly, the beauty of who you are extends from the center of Spirit to the soul, and from it to the mind, heart, body, and to everything that is part of your humanness.

These extensions of the pure holiness of your being reach your actions and all kinds of expressions or manifestations that emanate from you. For that reason, you are a link of light in a chain of holiness. In other words, every aspect of your life is imbued with who you are. Remember this joyfully.

Child of my divine heart, you have walked the path that led you to remember who you are. That brought you to these words. Rejoice, for you have found the priceless pearl, the lost drachma. Now begins the time when we tell our neighbors what we found, which we do by releasing our healing power. That is not the only way to share, but is the one that corresponds to you.

You have the power to heal yourself and to heal others, which is the same. Remember that on the plane of consciousness, that is, on the plane of truth, there is no such thing as "the outside and the inside," or "one and the other." In divine reality, and therefore in the only reality, everything is unity even though it manifests itself in infinite forms.

When the soul was created, whether human or not, it was given the grace of perpetual healing, the ability to sustain itself in health for all eternity. That capacity may have been denied as an invariable effect of the denial of being, but it exists. Remaining safe and sound is the reality of all aspects of creation. Does this not make sense?

Believing that a being outside of yourself can heal you but not you, yourself, is to believe that another has a power that you do not. If this were true, it would mean that in some way there must have been an unequal distribution in universal creation, giving some what is not given to others. An idea like this is so far from the truth that it totally denies the reality of love, for love makes no exceptions, ever. Everything is given to all, eternally.

The resurrection unlocked healing consciousness. By this I mean that after the universal awareness of the resurrection—something that happened on the level of form two thousand years ago with my divine expression as the risen Jesus—the power of souls to stay healthy and safe forever was released.

III. Everything of Mine Belongs to You

Although it is true that upon denying being you denied everything that is part of yourself—and with it the power to remain in truth and in perfect harmony in the life that flows eternally—nevertheless, the denial of something does not cause it to cease being. Does denying the beauty of a flower cause it to cease being? Can you see now why I have said in countless ways, through my many manifestations, to accept everything as it is?

To accept that you are the resurrected is to accept that everything that is part of me is also part of you. It cannot be otherwise, since all true creation is a perfect extension of that which gives it existence. Every creator, to be such, creates from himself, therefore it is impossible for something to exist in you that does not come from me, or vice versa.

I am the resurrection and the life. I said this long ago. Here I repeat it, for love. Your function now is to make it your only truth. That statement coming from my divine being is an expression of what you yourself are and will always be. You cannot be anything else because you are mine.

Perhaps you think that something or someone that is mine can be different from what I am, since in your experience of the world you believe you can possess things foreign to you. But remember, we are not considering the level of illusions, but the level of reality. In the Kingdom of Heaven, which is the true consciousness of creation, being and having are identical. Everything is united in the House of the Father of Lights. You know this, since you were created with that perfect knowledge.

Healing and staying safe and sound for all eternity is a power of the soul. I do not say "attribute" of the soul, since what you are has no properties or qualities. It simply is. Being is pure potentiality, pure power. Therefore, your being bears the power that allows you to resurrect to eternal life, that is, to return to the state of grace and remain in grace forever. In other words, it has the ability to be as it was created to be.

I demonstrated the truth revealed here when I manifested myself in the glory of my resurrection and in the glorious assumption of Mary. Death was never a part of me; I am life that has no end. I did not make that demonstration for myself to become aware, but because it was the perfect moment in which the realm of time was in a position to become aware of universal resurrection. The floodgates of the infinite healing power of Christ in humanity and in every living being were opened.

The source of the healing of the soul, that is, of the restorative power of its being, resides in unity. It cannot be found anywhere else; there is no such thing as something additional to your reality. Beyond divine union is nothing. Beyond truth is no life, no existence. Outside of me—because I am the Source of your true being and therefore am your being—there is no reality, no world, no creation. There is only one life, one holy being, a single eternity. In short, only one true God: love.

29.

In the Fullness of Union

I. Being One and Being Many

Blessed soul of your Heavenly Father and Mother, light emanating from true light, today I come full of joy for this time of dialogue of love and truth. With my heart overflowing with happiness, I thank you for your willingness to listen to my voice and receive my being, for your "yes" to love.

Listen, beloved ones, if you can only heal in unity, then the reality of that will surely remain in you, its home. Immerse yourself now in the memory of the sweet truth that we will now remember together, which will fill your soul with joy because of the memory of our union.

You live in me, as I do in you. I am both your home and your beloved guest. I am your sun, and you are a ray of light emanating from my being, not the other way around.

You may feel that what I just said contains an intrinsic contradiction. The mind will say: How is it possible that what is one is not the same? Can what is one also be many? Thoughts like this are typical of the old way of thinking, which is not in harmony with who you really are but is a mental pattern of the former being that you once thought you were but you will never be, since it is not true.

A mind that thinks in terms of separation believes that space is limited, therefore cannot conceive that I am your home and at the same time your guest. But if you put aside the limited, illusory self's way of thinking and remember joyfully that we are united, and that therefore what I am is also you, you can see that I am as much a guest of your soul as you are of my being. You are, because I am. You live in me, because I live in you.

When you recognize that I live in you, you also accept that everything lives in you, since I am the everything of everything. Therefore, it is unnecessary and untrue, to limit myself. Totality has no limits; by living in you, everything must dwell in you, including the infinite. This is how you become a guest of divinity. This is saying that you live in the House of Truth because it lives in your being.

On the other hand, my beloved, what I meant by saying "and not the other way around," is the same as when it was said that "as it is inside, it is also outside and not the other way around". Holy daughter, holy son, this is a loving reminder that you are my expression, the work of my hands, a beautiful ray of light that shines in all its glory, and whose Source is my divine heart. In other words, as it is in me, so it is in you, and never the other way around.

Rejoice in remembering that all that I am is you, and nothing that does not come from me can be part of you. Not now, not ever.

You may believe that if you are safe and sound and the healing power of your being has been unlocked and thus spreads freely, then you cannot experience physical illness or suffering. This belief does not make sense if you look at my example life, as well as that of my most holy mother, who is also yours.

II. Healing and Unity

Y ou can be a being living in the perfect state of Christ's healing, that is, in the resurrection, and still arrange for the restoration of the mystical body of Christ through the experience of what you call sickness, or even pain in any of its forms. That is, joining me in the resurrection—the only place where you can do it—forming part of my redemptive passion. It is evident that, in the world of opposites, this must be an available option, although its apparent opposite must also be.

After all, remember that you can only join me in the resurrection for there is nothing other than eternal life. Only in it are we united in being, the eternal reality of love. In other words, only in resurrection are you as you were created to be.

Did I stop being Christ because I chose the experience of the cross? Or did my mother not go through the experience of being equally crucified in spirit and truth? We both suffer the same because we are united. Even so, no experience in time could make us cease being what we are: the living expression of Christ in humanity—the masculine and feminine of God, if you prefer, although it would be more accurate to say duality united perfectly in love.

The term "healing" will be re-signified in the new, so we bring up this matter here. Although ultimately there will be no experience of pain in any of its forms, since the idea of separation will be completely abolished from the mind that thought it, the fact remains that there needs to be a transition from the current state of enlightenment to the attainment of fully enlightened human consciousness.

Frequently the path of healing includes bringing to the light of the consciousness of Christ what must be healed through human experience. That does not mean that when you do so you have disconnected from your healing power, or from your state of being safe and sound. It simply means that you are deploying that power in a particular way. There are many ways to heal. Walking the path of redemptive passion, taking to the cross everything untrue so it vanishes in a visible and eloquent way, is one way but not the only one.

Do not worry about what form of expression your healing power will take. Whatever it is, it will always be in perfect harmony with your will, and therefore with who you really are. Nothing that flows through you from now on will cease being a perfect extension of my divine being in you. Do not forget: You are as a beautiful ray of sunshine to the sun, always bright, always pure, always enlivening.

My beloved, I am not advocating the creation of a healing method here. How could I do that if healing is the effect of the life-giving force that flows from your being? If the source of healing is Christ, and I assure you this is eternally true, then healing cannot be just a form, but the essential being. Put another way, I seek not to create a method to heal others or yourself, but we are becoming aware that your being is itself the source of healing, as much as I am.

III. The Healed Identity

Being healing itself is different from establishing an external way to heal. It is about accepting the fact that when you unite with me—uniting with your true essence—you invoke the healing power that your being itself is. Just as when you turn on a light, the light dispels the darkness as an inherent effect of what it is, likewise when you remain joined with your being, you extend holiness, plenitude, wisdom, and everything else that it is. You cannot open the curtains on a sunny day without lighting up the room.

The way to unite with your essential being is to remember that Christ is your true identity in God, just as He is in every aspect of creation. Why is this important to remember? Because it is the only way to live fully. The soul perfectly embodies Spirit; it is an extension of what gives it life.

Since Spirit lives eternally in a state of perfection with its center or heart in Christ, consequently the soul carries within itself everything it needs to live a full, healthy, radiant, happy life eternally. Why have you often experienced the opposite? Because you had disconnected from your being—not in truth, but in illusion. You were living a life without being fully aware of the Christ in you.

I am life without end. Returning to me is the path to peace, harmony, and fulfillment. Just as you were told that you are holiness personified because I am the Source of holiness and am holiness itself, for the same reason you are now told that you are eternal life. Rejoice in this truth! Allow yourself to be accompanied always by its sweet voice, acknowledging to yourself:

I am eternal, I am healthy, I always have been and always will be. The truth about me is Christ. In union with him we are the eternal reality of love.

30.

Be Full

I. Pure Consciousness, Pure Love

In a way, "resurrection consciousness" is not the same as "the Christ consciousness in you." Although the term "consciousness" associated with any subject is somewhat inconceivable in truth since there is no quality in consciousness, nevertheless human language has attributed certain qualities to it in order to enhance comprehension, for sheer abstraction means little to the thinking mind which uses words because of its tendency to be concrete.

However, there is only one consciousness, and that is divine consciousness. That is, there is only one love and that is God. Or more precisely, you are pure consciousness. When you are aware of who you truly are, you live in pure consciousness. You participate in Christ consciousness. You live a real life. When you are not in true consciousness, you are immersed in an illusory life, unaware of truth.

You know, because you have been created with the knowledge that when you join with what you are, you feel peace, joy, and certainty, and therefore can live fully. That eternal knowing of your soul led you to seek me from an early age, even before you could formulate abstract philosophical thoughts. What brings you here now, reading these words? What moves you to do good because you feel peace in doing so? What prompts you to go to the temple to join me so often, or to seek the truth wholeheart-edly in books, encounters, rituals, and much more? It is because of what you are.

Your being knows everything and sees everything. It is perfect knowledge. It is infinite power in me, perfect wisdom in me, eternal reality in me. Outside of me it is nothing because there is no such thing as anything outside of me. Thus, nothing outside of you is true. By my living in you, you live in me and everything lives in us. We are the totality of love, the vast reality of infinite being. Truly, truly I tell you that you were not created for the eternal; rather, you are eternity, not "for" the infinite, but you are infinity.

We are now in a position to joyfully acknowledge and accept the following: Resurrection is not a state to be reached, nor is it a reward, it is what you are. It cannot be otherwise, since in you, as in me, there are no seams, parts, or divisions.

Our being is like a beautiful seamless garment, a sacred cloak that covers all creation with its beauty and holiness. The stars are painted on it; the sun too. In it exist the lives of men and women of all times, all living beings, and those yet to live. Every petal of every flower lives in our being. Every thought ever thought or yet to be thought dwells in its divine face—not those that look like thoughts but are not, but every expression of the pure thought of love that God is.

Because you are resurrection, you cannot help but have the ability to raise the dead, heal wounds, illuminate minds, and recreate the realm of time, space, and matter. The world of form and limitation is one in which everything can be transformed; there is not a single aspect of it that cannot be changed by your being. When we embrace the laws of change together in our being, the New Heaven and the New Earth are the result.

II. Holding Hands

Can you begin to glimpse how important it is to accept the resurrection in yourself? If you do not, the sonship cannot be resurrected, for we are united. Beloved of my divine heart, do not let this worry you. Remember, since we are united, it is enough for a single aspect of creation to accept what Heaven gives in order for all of it to receive it in unison, for giving and receiving are one outside of time, that is, in truth.

Therefore, since I have risen, being the first, you have risen with me. The only thing required of you now is your willingness, at least minimally, to receive the revelation that these words bring you from the abode of holy knowledge. You know that they are the voice of truth, an authoritative expression of divine knowledge. You know this because you know who is its divine Source.

In the depth of your souls, my beloved sons and daughters, all truth shines radiantly. In that impregnable space dwells what you call God, Being, Ultimate Reality. When you stay there you dwell in Heaven. By resting there you dwell in a peace that has no opposite. By immersing yourself in its crystalline waters, you become one with perfect knowledge. Worlds upon infinite worlds of love and holiness are eternally created and recreated within its limitlessness. The laughter of the angels of light adorns Her beauty in union with their eternal melodies of gratitude.

Oh, my beloved daughters and sons from all corners of the world, listen to what this Divine Mother, full of love for each of you and for all creation, comes to say. Receive this blessed work for what it is: a rain of blessings pouring from the Heaven of our only holy reality. Accept them like drops of dew that water the beauty of your hearts and lead them to greater love. I assure you, you will not regret it. Make each of the words that you receive here yours, for they are. You who listen to my voice and follow it, know that they were created from all eternity in the one mind and are as much yours as everyone's. They are an expression of the resurrection.

This revelation is a manifestation of a new wave of consciousness. It is an extension of divine consciousness in the form of human words. It is a ray of sunshine. It is like each of your holy hearts: a sun whose nucleus constantly emanates rays of holiness, wisdom, plenitude, infinite bliss, and life without end. That is why the light never goes out in the Kingdom of Heaven. In it the perpetual sun of life, which is Christ, gives life to each of your hearts. They are the blessed rays of Christ, always united to Source, to Reality.

III. Light of True Light

Can you now understand, child of my bosom, why so often in our dialogues of love and truth—most of which will never be read by any mind in this world—I have called you "sun of my sun," or "being of my being"? Just as each soul is like a ray that emerges from my being, so also each of them is called to be a sun of life.

Truly, truly I tell you that great rays flow from your being, extending to all creation with a beauty that surpasses all imagination. They cannot be seen with the eyes of the body but are seen with those of Spirit. It is a fact that everyone who walks or has ever walked the Earth sees them at some point. Perhaps they cannot put that experience into words, but they know how it feels. Everyone lives in the Heaven of perfect love. Carry the memory of this Heavenly statement in the silence of your heart and you will be accompanied by pure truth.

Receive now the resurrection prayer. Carry it imprinted in your heart. I assure you that the mind will rejoice in the peace of God, and the body will be illuminated. It will also help you anticipate the universal event of enlightenment of consciousness. In this way you will begin to live an eternal epiphany. You will be like God walking on Earth, just as I was when walking the paths of the world two thousand years ago, or as your Mother Mary was, in the perpetual joy of love.

I am the resurrected of love, the light that emanates from the eternal sun that Christ is. In me lives the life that has no end. I am forever safe and sound. I extend fullness. I am resurrection and life, always one with my being.

31.

My Voice Will Be Heard

I. Every Wound Will Heal

Beloved soul of Christ, here we are once again, reunited in the eternal reality of love. The voice that exists since before time began and gives life to everything is manifesting itself in these words. I am divine essence made human. This work is an unequivocal example of the union of Heaven and Earth. Everything is united. If you immerse yourself in its light, you will remember more vividly the One who is its divine Source. This will bring to you the memory of a love without beginning or end, the love you truly are.

This manifestation of Christ consciousness is in itself a path of healing, a medium for the healing of minds, bodies, and souls, both individually and collectively. Resurrection has the power to restore whatever needs restoration, to illuminate the darkened, and to sanctify what is disconnected from truth, reuniting with it.

What else could happen in the prelude to a new Heaven and a new Earth if not the total healing of creation? That is the natural step that precedes the fullness of the Second Coming of Christ, the Second Advent, the state of Christ consciousness freely expressing itself in all, not as the source of healing but as its perfect expression. In other words, Christ will not come to heal the sick, as he did in the First Coming, but will shine in all his glory and splendor on every created thing, for all healing will have been consummated.

Being aware of the resurrection that you really are is the means to reach the fullness of being because it is what constitutes your reality. You have never been beyond the light of resurrection. You have never lived apart from the love of God. You have been, and always will be, one with your Divine Mother. The mind may have dissociated itself to believe incredible things, but that does not change what you are.

Perhaps in your particular case the healing path has taken a specific form, or it does so in what you consider to be the future. Even so, that does not imply that you are not whole, or are disconnected from truth. It means only that you have shaped the formless, that you decided to manifest what existed in the depths of the unmanifest. Or in this case, that healing exists, it is desirable, and you have achieved it. That too has a purpose.

On the plane of duality, things cannot exist without their opposite; one gives existence to the other. Thus, healing cannot exist without its opposite. But the path we are walking gently leads you beyond this duality towards the one reality of God where opposites do not exist. If the thinking mind believes that understanding depends on drawing comparisons, healing will follow the path of duality. It will do so in order that you can become aware that you are already healthy, that you have already risen; in other words, that you are an eternal savior as well as the one saved, and so that you become fully aware that you shine forever in the glory of holiness.

II. A New Life

The resurrection is but the restoration of full consciousness of what you really are. The same applies to all creation. Being as God created is the reality of the soul, of every living being, and of every created thing. The power of the resurrection, which dwells in you as much as in everything that exists, gathers within the embrace of love everything that seemed to have separated from it. Thus the power to heal resides in you and in every creation.

We could say that resurrecting means to definitively awaken to truth. Was not that what I did when I came back from apparent death? In that universal event of consciousness, the dream of death and separation was abolished.

Let me say it clearly: The resurrection opened an imperishable channel or link between the human mind and that of Christ, and between the heart of every man and woman with that of the Mother of the living. Because of this, the bridge that unites human nature with divine nature was unlocked, along with everything created with its Source. In other words, Heaven returned to the unity it is with Earth. This did not occur in the reality of God, where they were always one, but in the singular consciousness of the created.

It is of little use that truth is bright and benevolent if you decide to live in the shadows and cruelty of unconsciousness, although that choice can be made, not in the realm of the divine but in the fantasies of a mind imagining things instead of embracing reality. Nevertheless, the effects of fear that such a belief entail will be experienced as real by a mind that believes that reality is devoid of intrinsic, loving meaning because it wants them to be. Why else would it harbor such nonsense? Remember, the separated mind believes that it can create its own reality, and it does so through fantasies.

Ceasing to fabricate illusions and living in a state in which the mind and heart, fully united, have been restored and have thus recovered their original condition, is itself the resurrection. Once the light of Christ illuminates the human soul in its experience of separation, the body and everything that is part of your humanness is reintegrated into truth.

III. Love Heals

You may wonder why a work that seeks to achieve total healing on both individual and collective levels offers so few concrete steps of a healing path. This question, my beloved, reveals that you still believe in the concepts of health, healing, disease, and unfulfillment as you did in the past, a way of thinking that is not part of the new consciousness already here. For the Holy Spirit, the true meaning of fullness has little or no relationship to your ideas about it, for fullness is expressed in every being that lives in truth, regardless of the path it travels.

Love is the fullness of life. Remember, all you need do is let yourself be loved, for with that, the life force of my divine heart will flow over you and extend beyond you to all creation. Above all, you will allow yourself to live in harmony with your being of pure holy love.

There is no cause for fulfillment other than love, because outside of your reality nothing is true. In the total absence of truth there can only be chaos, meaninglessness, lack of peace, and all other conditions contrary to holiness.

What kind of fullness could there be where there is nothing that comes from eternal perfection, that is, from God? You know the answer. Therefore, this work leads you to live in love as the

Source of access to the divine knowledge of what you are, and of eternal life.

Let us be silent for a few moments. Let my voice reach you. Refrain from judging. Let it remind you of what you are. Allow it to show you the great rays that emerge from the center of your being to all creation. Feel how it gently leads you back to the House of Truth, where you dwell safely forever in the arms of love. You will see that you are a new sun, born from the sun of life, one who extends beautiful rays towards its holy creations, just as Divine Mother does from Her being towards you. A sun has created a new sun. One love has created a new holy love. Mother and child merge in the light of holiness.

32.

Resurrect In Life

I. Resurrection Now

Beloved soul full of grace, light that illuminates the world, here we are again, united in the certainty of truth. What a joy it is to live in the union of the holy, beautiful, and eternally perfect! What joy our hearts feel as we come together in these sacred encounters, dialogues filled with the love and wisdom of Heaven!

I remind you once more, sons and daughters of my heart, that each time these conversations manifest as a living expression, the pure energy of the mind of Christ extends to all creation. A wave of divine light ripples through space and time, enveloping all matter and all non-material reality in its holiness.

Listen, being of my being, to what I next remind you of, for love. The message I gave to the world with my life in the lands of Jerusalem and its surroundings has been that of resurrection in life, not resurrection after death. If death does not exist, since it is not real and cannot be, how can a resurrection be an effect of it?

To believe that resurrection is linked to death is to misunderstand completely. You are not asked to die in order to rise again. You are invited to resurrect right now to the truth of who you are. This is something accomplished in life. I shall put it another way to satisfy the thinking mind's need for definitions, although not without first reminding you that every definition is simply a signpost that points to truth or illusion. Words are never the truth itself, which is beyond all symbols and limits.

You need not understand the resurrection; you know it perfectly through your consciousness. In the silence of your heart you know what I am speaking about. Nevertheless, here I will offer some words to help the thinking mind join the truth so desired and loved by all humanity.

Resurrecting in life means that you stop being the old and false being that once you thought you were, and begin to be the true being that you are forever. In other words, you die to the old and are reborn in the light of truth. Naturally, this does not require physical, human death. Death cannot bear any power; death is the idea of impotence taken to its maximum expression.

You can, and are called to, resurrect now and in every moment. This also needs clarification. Once you resurrect to truth, you cannot go back. So when I tell you "in every moment," I do not mean that you can go back to the level of consciousness you reached. You never go backwards. What is meant is that it is perfectly possible to be aware of the new being that you are. And since God is eternal renewal, you are a new holy creation in every moment.

II. Spirit Reborn

Remember, my daughter, my son, that love is the foundation of life and therefore of what you are. And since its power makes all things new, you cannot be static. You are living love, living being, always in vital movement, always expressing new life, new holy love.

One day I said: Dying to the world to realize that death does not exist is the path to truth. Today you can understand this sweet revelation in greater depth. I wanted to remind you that you have already risen to eternal life, since eternal life is what you really are.

Resurrection in life is about you as a unique being and all humanity as a universal family. Even beyond that, it includes all of creation. This is why a new humanity is being born. The profound changes in the world being experienced today are an expression of this.

My daughters and sons, love is enveloping you with all its light, benevolence, and holiness. It calls you to be reborn and you have answered its call. That is why you are no longer the old humanity you once were. A transformation of such magnitude cannot be understood from one day to the next by a mind accustomed to understanding things based on what it has learned in the past.

Resurrecting in life is leaving behind the being that was grounded in the illusion of the ego—a false being that created an experience of selfishness, idolatry of the fleeting, the search for power to satisfy the desire to be special and feel superior, as well as the false need for accumulation to fill a void that can be filled only by love. Resurrecting in life is also to embrace forever the truth of what you are: a holy being, born from the core of holiness, who lives eternally in unity with your divine Source.

When you recognize the truth of who you are and live in unity with it, you are living in resurrection consciousness, and what is more, you are being resurrection itself because you are life. If this is true, and I assure you that it is, you cannot be resurrected in death, but only in life. Remember, nothing is achieved by annihilation or denial. Everything that the holiness of your being can do, it does in life because only eternal life is real.

I shall say in another way what is remembered here: Living in harmony with the being that you really are is resurrection. Do you need to die to be who God created you to be? I answer this question with a yes and a no. You needed to die to the old self that once you wanted to be, which has nothing holy, beautiful, or loving about it. Although it is not a real death, it is experienced as such. That was where the pain of transformation came from, what some call the dark night of the soul, or the birth pains of the Christ in you.

III. Risen Now

I said I would answer with a yes and a no. On the plane of truth, the false self that seemed to die never died because it was never born. It did not fade because it was never real. Indeed, that false self is nothingness. It has no substance and never had. Therefore, it only seemed real in your imagination, in a feverish mind that harbored illusions, hoping to be a creator of itself in a way far removed from God's way of creating.

You need not die to be who you really are. Be glad that this is true. Rejoice as you remember together that the call to you today, just as mine was two thousand years ago, is to rise alive and reborn from Spirit, that is, from above. Let yourself be carried away by the breath of my love—you know now where it comes from and where it goes. It comes from my divine heart and it leads you to it. In other words, it comes from Heaven and goes to Heaven, in union with your being.

Truly, truly I tell you, beloveds from all corners of the world, that the new humanity is already here. Soon the painful memory of a life lived outside of union with Christ will be gone. First it will be a painful memory, then just a little one, and finally a total forgetting of the experience of separation.

The world will not succumb. It will be transformed into love. It will be reborn from above. It will do so as an inevitable effect of my resurrection—the reunion of singular consciousness with the divine. The universe will return to the state of unity wherein the light of Christ will reflect undistorted.

Do not worry about the mental musings that this revelation can cause in the thinking mind, questioning a number of things. Rather, bring what has been shared here to the present in your heart, the only place where the reality of what you are resides in perfect union with your divine Source, in the timeless now where together we live forever in the unity of love.

Do that, and you will remember, not with cerebral memory but with spiritual memory which dwells in your consciousness, that you are resurrection and life. You will remember God because the memory of who you are will shine in your mind, your heart, and all your humanity, in the glory of truth. You will extend life. You will bring Heaven to Earth and you will contemplate the most valuable of the treasures of creation: your being, because you will be contemplating the Christ of God.

33.

Come, Blessed of My Being

I. Universal Love

Blessed soul, joy of my Divine Heart, daughter, son of holy light! Today I come full of joy to engage with you again in our dialogues of wisdom and love. These holy conversations come from the union of our hearts, beating in unison in harmony and truth. Receive with loving attention and innocent expectation what is remembered now for the good of many.

Saying that only love is real is the same as saying that only God is. His divine reality is the only Source of everything that exists. He alone is the causeless origin. This is something the thinking mind can accept with some ease. However, this apparent acceptance is not total if it still harbors the idea that death exists.

Truly, truly I tell you, that if you believe that the end of your life, or of any being, is to fade into nothingness, you have not fully embraced truth. Death does not exist. It has no consequences. Only eternal life is real because life is itself God. Absorb these words into your heart. Let them infuse your humanity. Immerse yourself in their purity and beauty.

In the depths of your soul, most holy being, is the perfect knowledge that what is being remembered here is pure truth. I am the Source of endless life. There is nothing in me other than perfect love. Therefore, nothing can spring from me that is not holy eternity. I say holy, not because there is another quality of the eternal, but so that you abandon the idea that what is not love can last. It cannot.

Does what cannot proceed from my divine being have a cause? And if not, where does it come from and where does it go? Here the mind can argue that, for what is not love, perhaps its origin is not its destiny, that a kind of split can be created in the eternal, something like the creation of a world where whatever does not come from me can live. Perhaps you believe that this would be an act of justice or a respect of freedom. But beloved ones, such a thing is impossible.

On what basis would love create what is not loving, holy, beautiful, and kind, if it can only create from itself? Remember, only God creates. Creatures cannot create by themselves; it is only possible to create in union with the Creator. As I have already said in other revelations, only love creates. Therefore, only the loving creations born from my divine reality are real.

I assure you that divine justice cannot be compared to human justice. Your criteria of what is fair or unfair, although they have their origin in perfect knowledge—otherwise you could not even conceive the idea of justice—are as far from divine truth as everything else that has been devised in the thought system of separation.

II. I Have Given You Eternal Life

What is fair in God is that His creations dwell with Him because that is His divine will. They belong to Him; they are an extension of His holy reality. This cannot be eliminated from the soul because everything created carries within itself the impulse to exist or it would not be.

What is fair in perfect love is that everyone enjoys the eternal plenitude that constitutes their origin and destiny. Therefore, everyone has a right to Heaven; it is a birthright. The joyous acceptance of this truth is the last distance that needs to be traveled before reaching the gates of the Heavenly Kingdom—there, where I wait for you with open arms, together with all holy creations.

Put another way, resurrection in life is a gift to you because of what you are. Everyone has a right to it because of what love gives to everyone without distinction. That certain daughters and sons are asleep to the truth or remain in a state of ignorance of their true being, does not mean that this need be the case forever. It can be changed. This is why the world of changes has been created, so that everyone in it can remember what they really are, and thus remember God. In doing so, they inevitably return to the eternal abode. How or when that happens is a matter for each soul in union with God.

Undoubtedly, there is a need for the transmutation of rooted patterns that are disengaged from love, both mentally and emotionally, before one can choose in truth. That is something that can be done in this world of time and space, form and modification. But it is not the only way. There are many others. The divine mind is infinite and does not limit itself when creating gifts that allow its sons and daughters to remain in the light of eternal life.

In the end, my daughters and sons, everyone will choose love. That will be the triumph of truth. They will do so because when the eyes of their spirits are opened, they will remember divine reality and will fully understand that there is only one option: God, who has no opposite. Instantly the soul will understand that the choice is between being or not being—that is, embracing eternal life or ceasing to exist. There is no third option. It will also recognize that of those two options, only one is real. The other will disappear from sight as it is illusory. Finally, in that state of consciousness, the soul will unite with its deepest desire to be, and will see the only possible option: to live forever in the arms of love.

Remember, my daughter, my son, that the freedom of the children of God really has nothing to do with choosing between options, since perfect love has no opposite. Only love is true. And remember, no one can sleep forever; that is impossible. Therefore, it follows that in the end all will awaken to the truth, some earlier, others later.

Returning to love or awakening to Christ consciousness, which are the same, can be done now, without delay, by letting yourself be carried away by the breath of the Holy Spirit and thus being reborn. Truly I tell you, the sweetness of its divine love transmutes within you everything needing to be transmuted: coal becomes gold and illusion gives way to truth. Ultimately this is the resurrection.

Resurrecting is something as inherent to your being as love. This is because divine power sustains all its creations in eternal life. Now let us connect the dots.

True freedom consists in doing your will. True justice means allowing that to happen forever. However, those who sleep the dream of oblivion do not remember who they are or what their true will is. They don't know what they want nor what they do. Living in such a state, they believe that their will can be and has been separated from the divine will. However, when the soul awakens to truth, it recognizes that its will and that of its Source are one and the same. And with that, it no longer wants to be without God, just as God does not want to be without His daughters and sons.

III. For Me, Nothing Is Impossible

Perhaps you wonder when or how the awakening of consciousness to the truth being revealed here occurs. Beloved holy being, this happens when it has to happen as the soul has arranged in union with its Creator, for resurrecting means awakening to perfect love's unique reality.

Now I ask you not to get lost in generalities. We have traveled a path full of light, revealing and remembering truth. We did so because what is true for you from all eternity is also true for the whole world. There is no such thing as separation—one and the other. All my children are equally loved, equally holy, equally worthy of resurrection.

Do not worry about how each soul makes its way to the ultimate embrace of love. Simply trust that my divine power and infinite wisdom know how to guide each of its holy creations, including yourself.

You are not being asked to accept a new belief regarding life and death, or damnation and eternal bliss. You are simply being asked to be willing to accept, at least for a moment, that the resurrection of the son of God is not something done for myself alone, but for everyone and everything. It is, therefore, a gift given to you. Accept it as your only reality and you will be accepting the will of God.

If all reality lives in Christ, and I assure you this is eternally true, you have to live in him as much as he lives in God, by being one with him. Therefore, the resurrection to eternal life must be as much yours as his. Remember, your will is to be, which is the same as saying you want to live the real life. You want endless bliss. In other words, you want to live forever in me, as much as I must live forever in you.

My beloveds, you who listen to my voice and follow it, you who have dedicated your time and humanity to receive these words of wisdom and truth, receive the gift of prayer that I give you below. Make it a litany in your life. Be accompanied by the grace it bears. By doing so, you come closer to me. You become more aware of the love that surrounds you on all sides. Do this with joy and with an eye toward the glorious day when our burning hearts will burst into new light.

Divine Heart, Source of my being. I thank you for the gift of resurrection. I accept it with all my love. I gladly receive it. And because I receive it, I give it, in the happy recognition of the truth about me. I am eternity, stretching out forever in the light of Christ. I am a being of holiness.

I am the resurrected of love.

Final words

Blessed son, daughter of my divine being, soul that hears and follows the voice of love, I tell you: Be glad you arrived at this part of the road. You are on sacred ground. You have reached the state where the truth of who you are will begin to manifest in a new light. It will shine in an increasingly radiant, brighter, and more beautiful way. The luminescence of the holiness that you are will bear witness to your resurrection to eternal life.

You who have risen in life, know that the choice to embrace eternity has already been made in the depth of your heart. You have chosen the best part and it will not be taken from you. Now it remains for us to call our brothers and sisters to join us in resurrection, the only place where we can truly unite.

Being of my being, I give you my love, and with it, eternal life. Accept it as a most holy offering of my divine heart. I am the origin of all creation, Source of wisdom, cause of all that is holy, beautiful, and perfect, cause of joy for souls who live in the truth, destiny of creation, and abode of light and peace.

Oh, soul full of beauty! You have no idea how far you have come on the path of light. Here we are, united in a love without beginning or end. Hand-in-hand we walk the paths of the world together. We bring the resurrection to all who are already ready to receive it, and also to those who are not yet ready but will be, because of our call to life.

I say to you who receive these words, accept them in your heart for what they are: messages from the Christ in you who loves you with a love without opposite. From all eternity I have created these messages so they would reach your hands at the perfect moment. Together let us give thanks to this friendly hand, a pencil in the hands of love, who with holy devotion surrenders to his role as Heaven's scribe, with the sole purpose that my voice becomes a human word so it can reach you who are the light of my being.

To all my sons and daughters around the world, this is an invitation to go beyond what has been learned, towards the truth that is beyond all definitions and symbols, where the perfect knowledge of what you are dwells, coming from God.

Let yourselves be led to the holy dwelling place of your being in Christ. There you will remember who you are. In doing so, you will recognize the perfect unity that exists between your being and your divine Source. That memory will bring Heaven to Earth and give you the bliss you long for in the depth of your holy heart.

I extend this invitation for you to take the last step on the path towards awakening to truth: Accept the resurrection now. That is, allow yourself to be gently led by Spirit and reborn from On High. I assure you, He who makes all things new will give you new life in every moment. You will leave behind everything that made you suffer. You will embrace forever, from now on, the lasting joy and peace of Heaven. Truly, truly I tell you that whoever allows himself to be transformed by love will inherit the Earth.

My beloved, go into the world bringing the resurrection wherever my love sends you. Let yourself be flooded by my light. Immerse yourself in the holiness of your being. Abandon yourself totally in me who Am the Source of beautiful love, and you will see great wonders in your life, now and forever. Make love the only source of your knowledge and action.

I bless you in my divine being.

Jesus, the Christ in You

About the Receiver

Sebastián Blaksley is a native of Buenos Aires, Argentina, born in 1968 into a large traditional Catholic family. He attended the Colegio del Salvador, a Jesuit school head-mastered by Jorge Bergoglio, the current Pope Francis. Although he wanted to be a monk as a young man, Sebastián's family did not consider it acceptable, and the inner voice that he always obeyed spoke thus: "You must be in the world, without being of the world." He studied Business Administration in Buenos Aires and completed his postgraduate studies in the U.S. He held several highly responsible positions in well-known inter-national corporations, living and working in the U.S., England, China, and Panama. He then founded a corporate consulting firm in Argentina that he led for 10 years. Sebastián has two daughters with his former wife.

At the age of six, Sebastián was involved in a near-fatal accident during which he heard a voice, which later identified itself as Jesus. Ever since he has continued to hear this voice. Sebastián says: "Since I can remember, I have felt the call of Jesus and Mary to live surrendered to their will. I am devoted to my Catholic faith."

In 2013, he began to record messages from his mystical experi-ences. In 2016 he miraculously discovered *A Course of Love* and felt the call to devote himself to bringing it to the Spanish-speaking world. He also now receives, transcribes, and shares what the voice of Christ—the voice of love—dictates. Most recently he has received and shared *Choose Only Love*, a series of seven books.

Sebastián is the president of the nonprofit Fundación Un Curso de Amor, www.fundacionamorvivo.org, through which he shares *A Course of Love* and *Choose Only Love*.

Works Received through Sebastián Blaksley

The Choose Only Love series
Choose Only Love: Echoes of Holiness (Book I)
Choose Only Love: Let Yourself Be Loved (Book II)
Choose Only Love: Homo-Christus Deo (Book III)
Choose Only Love: Wisdom (Book IV)
Choose Only Love: The Holy Dwelling (Book V)
Choose Only Love: The Divine Relationship (Book VI)
Choose Only Love: The Way of Being (Book VII)

The Truly Beloved Series
Truly Beloved: Love Letters from the Divine Mother in You (early 2024)
Truly Beloved: Love Letters from the Christ in You (mid-2024)
Truly Beloved: Love Letters from an Angel (late 2024)

Other Key Works
The Age of the Heart: The Birth of a New Heaven and a New Earth
Resurrection Consciousness: Portal to Universal Enlightenment

All works are available as audiobooks on Audible.com, Amazon.com, and iTunes.
Audiobooks of *Choose Only Love* narrated in Spanish by Sebastián Blaksley are available on www.beek.io.

The website http://cocreatingclarity.org/CHOL/ offers a powerful search tool that enables searches for words or phrases within all of the *Choose Only Love* books.

The website https://www.chooseonlylove.org offers free chapters and other resources about the Choose Only Love books, the Refuge of Divine Love in Argentina, the Way of Being program, the Hour of Grace program, additional information about Sebastián Blaksley, and more.

Information about the Spanish-language books received by Sebastián, *Elige solo el amor*, and the companion book *Mi diálogo con Jesús y María: un retorno al amor* is available at www.fundacionamorvivo.org

Other Works from Take Heart Publications

A Course of Love is a living course received from Jesus by
Mari Perron. It leads to the recognition, through experience, of
the truth of who we really are as human and divine beings—a
truth much more magnificent than we previously could
imagine. *A Course of Love* has been published in 10 languages
as of 2024. For more information go to www.acourseoflove.org.

Dewdrops of Wisdom: Practical Guidance from Mother Mary,
received by Marietta Beregi. In this important work Mother
Mary emerges not only as a being of great wisdom but also
as a supremely practical mother, fully compassionate
of human desires and foibles. This volume demonstrates
again and again her tender embrace and the importance of
relationships in spiritual awakening.